Who
Speaks
to Your
Heart?

Who
Speaks
to Your
Heart?

Tuning In to Hear God's Whispers

stacy hawkins adams

ZONDERVAN®

ZONDERVAN.com/
AUTHORTRACKER
follow your favorite authors

ZONDERVAN

Who Speaks to Your Heart?
Copyright © 2010 by Stacy Hawkins Adams

This title is also available as a Zondervan ebook. Visit www.zondervan.com/ebooks.

This title is also available in a Zondervan audio edition. Visit www.zondervan.fm.

Requests for information should be addressed to:

Zondervan, *Grand Rapids, Michigan 49530*

Library of Congress Cataloging-in-Publication Data

Adams, Stacy Hawkins, 1971–
    Who speaks to your heart? : tuning in to hear God's whispers / Stacy
Hawkins Adams.
        p.   cm.
    ISBN 978-0-310-29271-5 (softcover)
    1. Listening—Religious aspects—Christianity. 2. Spirituality. I. Title.
BV4647.L56A33   2010
248.8'43—dc22   2010004895

Cover design: Studio Gearbox
Cover photography: Veer
Interior design: Michelle Espinoza

Printed in the United States of America

---

10 11 12 13 14 15 /DCI/ 21 20 19 18 17 16 15 14 13 12 11 10 9 8 7 6 5 4 3 2 1

*To women everywhere
who yearn to recognize God's voice,
to serve the Creator more fully,
and in the process, to embrace their authentic selves.*

Contents

Part 4: Hearing God

Introduction

Years ago when I was trying to decide whether my dream of becoming a professional writer was a long shot for a shy, small-town southern girl, God spoke to my heart that since he had placed the desire there, it was a worthy calling to pursue. Never mind that I didn't personally know authors or journalists who could guide me to success, and never mind the doubt I sometimes encountered when I shared my aspirations with others. Very few people openly questioned my goals, but in some of their expressions I read their disbelief—the kind of disbelief one possesses when a petite child declares plans to play professional basketball, or an off-key singer (like myself) insists she'll be the next big musical sensation.

God didn't speak to me through a burning bush or through an angel bearing a scroll. There was just this ... *knowing*, this belief that he wouldn't have planted seeds inside me that he didn't intend to nurture. This confidence blossomed as I grew older and matured in my faith. I learned to make time to *listen* to God after I prayed and to find the courage to hear what God was saying—to my spirit, through other people, and through his divine Word, the Bible.

For every person who expressed doubt about my career

choice, there was another who read my poems, short stories, and articles and believed that my words were entertaining or inspiring enough to be shared with the world. They urged me to keep writing, to dream big, and to do whatever it would take to succeed. Those voices served as guideposts along my path, helping me move forward whenever I questioned my abilities and whether my goal was practical. They also provided the encouragement I needed to trust my feelings: I came alive when I put words and characters on paper. I knew I had to honor what I was experiencing.

I had been involved in church my entire life and had publicly declared my belief in Christ the summer I turned eight, but during my teens, I found myself more curious than ever about the Bible and the answers it might hold for my modern-day life. I remember wondering how Scriptures written so long ago could be relevant to anything I was facing in high school.

Sure, I was active in my church, and I prayed regularly. I believed that Jesus loved me. Yet I wrestled with what loving him back would cost me and with whether I would have the courage to give up, or pursue, whatever God might ask of me. I struggled to wrap my brain around messages in the Bible that declared that a God I couldn't see or touch had the time and interest to single me out from the millions of other people who wanted love, attention, and help. And if he *were* willing to do that, I wondered why — what made me special enough to be noticed? What makes any of us that valuable?

I discovered that when I sincerely asked him which of the paths I was considering would please him, the more I received his guidance. The more I allowed him to lead me, the more I began to know his voice.

These days, when I look back on that long-ago period of questioning, and when I consider the mountaintop and valley experiences that God has consistently shared with me, I'm humbled to realize in just how many ways he has spoken throughout my life, even when I wasn't ready to pinpoint him as the source. God's wisdom now guides me so often as a busy wife, mother, and writer that I am surprised by the wonder I feel when I see his fingerprints on my life. I have learned to trust that he's always working on my behalf no matter how things look, yet I'm still occasionally caught off guard by how creatively he does it.

Most of what others consider lucky breaks, fortunate circumstances, wishes granted, or even miracles, are kisses from God. These blessings are reminders that our hopes, our dreams, and even our fears and frustrations are safe with our heavenly Creator.

When no one else can relate to the days you want to hide out under the covers until a storm passes, or shout from the rooftops when you've achieved a sought-after accomplishment, or press a rewind or fast-forward button to shift your life from a period of stagnation or uncertainty, God is gently tapping on your heart's door. He's sending messages through the Scriptures, through strangers, and in numerous other ways to remind you that he is ever loving and ever present, ready and willing to speak to your need or your situation.

I've taught myself in recent years to close my eyes and picture a large-scale map of the world, spread out on a table.

I am standing at one end of the table, peering at this map from all angles. In some other regions of the world, I see people who are hungry and hopeless and believe they have no power to change their circumstances except through violence. In others, I see pain and prosperity mixed with pleas for relief, greedy actions, or prayers for salvation. I imagine that God wants to heal and help us all.

I tell myself that he is standing guard over this "map," and he sees my life and the world at large from every angle.

He has the perspective, the knowledge, and the power to know how best to protect me, teach me, comfort me, and mature me, because he knows how his plans for me can also impact his "child" down the block or in another part of the universe. He knows how the choices and circumstances someone else is dealing with can help me fulfill my purpose. This exercise teaches me to slow down, to stop fretting, and to trust that Romans 8:28 is correct: "In all things God works for the good of those who love him, who have been called according to his purpose."

Our role is to discipline ourselves to be real with God about who we are and where we are in life. It is to be still enough to not only pray to him, but also to watch and wait and listen with our hearts as well as with our ears for whatever messages or answers he chooses to send. Our role is to be in tune enough, or in a solid enough relationship with God, to respond to his direction, trusting that even when we don't understand, we know that God has already figured things out.

As you read this book for inspiration, insight, and

practical ideas on how to hear God speaking, prepare to feel a little uncomfortable when you recite the prayers or apply the tips and suggestions offered at the end of each chapter. The process of change and growth often leaves us uneasy. However, I've witnessed and experienced firsthand how venturing beyond familiar territory can open the vault to blessings that leave you speechless, and even lead you to purpose and destiny.

My personal journey of faith is woven throughout this book, simply as a model for how God can speak into an individual life when one is ready to hear and willing to embrace his response. As you read it, consider how the experiences I share (my own and others') relate to your life and your circumstances. Ask God to speak to you through these pages and to give you answers that fit your particular needs. Don't be afraid to let your thoughts wander, for it is in the quiet moments, when your heart is open and when you aren't trying so hard to squeeze the truth out of him, that God whispers wisdom that can settle your soul and bring you peace. You may or may not hear God speaking to you in the exact same manner as I or the other women featured in this book have heard him. However, the more often you practice listening, the more you will recognize his voice and know where he is leading. Then, my friend, it's your job to trust that voice and follow it!

part 1

Preparing Your Soul

I visited a small farmer's market with a friend a few months ago and wandered through the aisles browsing before I settled on what to buy. I paused at a booth selling black-berries and immediately pulled my wallet from my purse — not because I'd been purposely searching for this fruit, but because they reminded me of home, of a blackberry bush I had eaten from as a child in my grandmother's backyard. My young relatives and I played with abandon in those days and took the berries for granted, thinking they'd always be there. Eventually that bush withered and died, but the memories have lingered, as have memories of the other fruits and veg-etables Mama Ruby planted and eventually served from the dinner table.

Her tomatoes, squash, and cucumbers flourished. So did her houseplants, which she talked to lovingly each day as she watered them. Occasionally I would ask her why she chatted with inanimate objects, and each time she patiently explained that plants require love and attention as well as water. She was tending to their soil, but also to their being.

Mama Ruby didn't talk to the vines and leaves in her garden, but she made sure they were nurtured as well, pulling weeds from the dirt, adding nutrients as necessary, and keeping the patch of garden moist. She knew that if she didn't invest the energy upfront, there was no need to expect a good crop months down the road.

Our efforts to hear from God must begin in much the same way. We can't decide on a whim that we're going to listen more fully and expect that simply because we've made this declaration, the heavens will open and God will give us all the answers we need that very day. The leap from fear to faith, from worry to peace, or from shame to self-confidence takes routine effort, sincere prayers, and time. Yes, time and more time.

Just as my grandmother prepared her garden for harvest and spoke life to her plants, we have to prepare our soil — our spirits and souls — to receive all that God wants to give us. It is a multistep process.

The first step is to decide you want to know God better. Once you make that decision, you have to act on it. Schedule time to read the Bible five or more minutes a day, or consider participating in a weekly Bible study and ask God to reveal himself to you. As you study God's Word and begin to understand his character, you have to be honest about *your* character and about the areas of your life that need God's touch. This task isn't the same as creating a checklist of your faults or sins, for the sake of condemning yourself. Instead, it is requiring yourself to get still enough to candidly examine any attitudes, actions, and words that are keeping you from nurturing the spirit of God that yearns to blossom inside you. It is finding the courage to ask God to expose and heal the areas that are keeping you from growing beyond your current existence into a more fulfilling life.

Each step will draw you closer to God. You'll begin to learn his likes and dislikes and understand what pleases him and what breaks his heart.

The more you know about him, the more you'll learn to love and trust him. The more you love and trust him, the more you will seek him and recognize his voice when he whispers to your soul.

1

Who Is Speaking to Your Heart?

I am the mother of a middle school–age daughter. Yes, please pray for me! I say that partly in jest, but mostly because if you have raised or spent much time with teenagers or preteens, you know firsthand that nearly everything you do or say is an embarrassment to them. If I'm driving down the road singing along to a song on the radio, I embarrass my daughter because someone in a car traveling nearby might see me. If we're in a restaurant and I ask the waitress to correct a problem with my meal, she's mortified that I've drawn attention to myself, and thereby to her. She can't wear the same jeans or T-shirt to school or camp within a ten-day span because one of her friends will remember, and if she misses the premiere of a made-for-TV movie she's been longing to see, the world might stop rotating.

My little woman leaves me exasperated many a day, but when I'm on the brink of losing my patience, I remember taking my own mother through most of the same changes. Don't let God fool you—he has a sense of humor. Revenge (or vengeance) does belong to him, but if you're a parent, you'll find that he reaps it on your parents' behalf through *your* children. Just as I'm about to launch into a speech to my daughter about the foolishness of peer pressure and wanting to be like everybody else, a memory flashes across my mind's eye of some of the things I said and did to Mama that now explain why she spent so much time at her bedside, on her knees in prayer, every morning and evening.

What's clearly going on with my daughter is what development experts will tell you is normal: the rank of who influences her is gradually shifting from her parents to her peer group. That means that what her friends say and think means more to her on some days than what her dad and I insist is the truth. She eventually acknowledges that we're right, but other voices continue seeking to speak into particular areas of her life. In part, I think this shift of influence is inevitable, but I also see an opportunity. What better time than now to begin giving her the skills that this book seeks to equip you with—the tools to know God so intimately that *he* reigns supreme, no matter what else or who else aims to become first priority?

Regardless of whether you've acknowledged it, someone is influencing your actions and thoughts too. Stop for a moment and consider whose opinion you respect most. Is it your spouse's or a friend's? A parent's or other relatives'? Your colleagues' or a boss's? Often our immediate response to a question like this is to frown and say, "Please! I think for myself!" But really think about it: we live in a culture that thrives on "faking it until you make it," and being in the good graces of the "right people at the right time." Thin is still in and so are wealth and youthfulness. Fashion is celebrated, while faith in God is dismissed or ridiculed.

When I was a high school and college student, fitting in was a priority for me too. Having the right clothing and hairstyle mattered. The pop culture of that day, and the opinions of my friends, were speaking into my life. Then I realized I was in love, and while I had long been a Christian and prayed to God for guidance, my special friend's opinions came to matter a great deal. I also had to contend with the opinions and advice of my family, my college instructors, and my summer internship bosses.

To the outside world, I was clearly a go-getter—a journalism major with strong language skills and an ability to focus and achieve my academic and extracurricular goals with excellence. Inside, however, I wasn't much different than my daughter. Behind my smile and the confident execution of my academic and journalistic pursuits, I was a shy people-pleaser, and I wanted to be well liked as much as anybody.

I never compromised my values or my faith, and in fact I sometimes found myself estranged from acquaintances because I wouldn't just "go with the flow." But others' views still mattered, and I wanted to honor the adults in my life by making them proud or by proving through my devotion or hard work that I was worthy of their love and attention. I told myself that this was my practice with God too.

During that period, when I was acing college, soaring as a budding writer, holding steady in a long-time, long-distance romance, and publicly living out my Christian beliefs through regular church attendance and restraint from some of the college partying and pranks I had access to, I thought I had it all together. I could see that God was leading me and opening doors at every turn.

God was indeed blessing my hard work; but I also was holding tightly onto the reins. I was following the rules of what it meant to be a "good" Christian to the letter. I sought to hear loved ones and friends say "well done," rather than risk making a mistake, appearing foolish, or failing to follow what everyone else considered the logical path to pursue after college. Not that I had any rebellious temptations in mind, but had they been there, I wouldn't have veered far from what seemed a likely route to success.

I look back at that season of my life with the proverbial 20/20 vision that history gives us, and I can see that while I uttered routine prayers to God for wisdom and guidance, I didn't always have the courage to listen for his answers. Instead, I filled the times during which he would have gladly spoken with answers of my own or with the advice and directives from people I trusted and admired. They shared from the heart, but I wasn't wise enough in that season to realize that I should have paired the wisdom they offered with some quiet time alone with God to sort out just how he wanted me to move forward given all of the opportunities before me.

Over the course of this book, you'll likely find yourself reflecting on similar periods in your own life, when your excitement or impatience led you to hear what you wanted rather than waiting for God to speak. You'll have opportunities to acknowledge those circumstances and make a decision to learn from them rather than beat yourself up. With God's help, it's never too late to replace questionable patterns or habits with new ones that permit God to be your first responder.

Ultimately, for every situation we have questions about, there are divine answers. God doesn't always speak when we want him to, or how we want him to, but until we learn to listen for the unexpected and to look for the answers in whatever forms he sends them, we'll often miss the message or discover it later than necessary.

This book will give you practical steps to help you listen and hear God speaking. God rarely shouts or appears today as he did to Moses, in a burning bush. He doesn't routinely send angels to rouse us from our sleep and issue instructions as he did in biblical times. Wouldn't it be great if he did? We'd have no doubt that we were on the right track, and when doubt tried to delay us, we'd have tangible proof that God had given direction. But since we don't have that kind of road map, hearing him speak will require that we listen to our own lives so that we can learn to embrace all that God has created us to be. When we are in tune with who we are, we can better determine who God is to us. We'll have the guts to turn down the volume of life's chitter chatter and open ourselves up to him.

God often speaks in whispers — in subtle swishes through our mind or heart, through comments that seem perfectly timed from a friend or stranger, or in passages in a book, magazine, or website that touch our core. As we come to know his voice, we'll more often recognize him whenever and however he approaches us.

Becoming intimate with God will take time and commitment. It is a never-ending process that ebbs and flows with every season of life. This book can be considered a baby step in the right direction. But each step matters, especially if it brings you closer to the divine Creator. Decide that you want to hear from *him* rather than from everyone or everything else that's clamoring for first place in your life.

When you are certain you are ready to give God that primary position, tell him so, and let your actions back up your words. Make time in your schedule to study the Bible each day, even if only for a few minutes. Carve out time for more than just a mad-dash morning prayer and really talk to God instead of simply sharing your wish list with him. Ask him to help you learn how to quiet your mind and spirit so you can hear him speaking. Over time, prepare to be blessed.

Learning to Listen

Matthew 6:33: "But seek first his kingdom and his righteousness, and all these things will be given to you as well."

1 Thessalonians 5:17: "Pray continually."

Meditate on these Scriptures over the next few days and memorize them. Read the entire chapters of Matthew 6 and Thessalonians 5 to understand the full context in which this advice was rendered. Once you have memorized the verses, turn them into personal prayers, such as, "Lord, help me to seek your kingdom first and trust that you will provide everything else I need," and, "God, please help me pray throughout the day, trusting that you will guide my every word and action in ways that bring me closer to you."

2

Walk Before You Run

If you grew up in the seventies like me, or if you watch syndicated reruns of TV sitcoms, you may be familiar with *I Dream of Jeannie*. This quirky comedy, starring actress Barbara Eden, was based on the premise that a handsome astronaut, played by actor Larry Hagman, had a personal genie who could grant his wishes in seconds.

As an elementary-age child, I laughed at the actors' antics while mentally listing some of the things I would request if I had a genie: a later bedtime, good grades on all of my tests, a new bike, and a puppy. With one or two blinks from my genie, life would change for the better.

I soon learned that real life doesn't mirror TV, and that hard work brings you rewards faster than making wishes ever will. Eventually, I also came to understand that successes achieved without Christ's stamp of approval weren't quite as sweet. Yet even in adulthood there are days when life becomes so frantic or frustrating that my friends and I commiserate over our inability to snap our fingers or press a remote control to fix it all. If we could, who among us wouldn't be tempted to use the services of a personal assistant to help us achieve our goals, prepare dinner, and keep the house clean?

More importantly, what if we could somehow tap into God's thoughts and feelings? Wouldn't it be amazing to get his audible opinion about the decisions we're wrestling with or the relationships we're pursuing? Or how about his verbal guidance on which paths will steer us closer to achieving our dreams, help us become fulfilled in our relationships, and draw us closer to him?

But God grants us the freedom to shape the lives he has given us. Instead of demanding our devotion, he gives us the choice to deepen our relationship with him or veer to the seemingly greener grass offered by a life that limits the pursuit of God. If we're going to serve him, he doesn't want it to be because mama or grandmama made us. He's not interested in puppets or robots; worship is a decision, not a directive.

When I was twenty-two, I was a grown-up "baby" who thought I knew it all. I married my high school sweetheart, landed a great job as a newspaper reporter, and settled into a wonderful church community in Virginia where I formed friendships with many individuals and couples who would become like extended family. As I had during my childhood and my tenure in college, I delved right in, teaching a high school Sunday school class with my new husband, joining several church committees, and never missing a worship service unless I was sick or out of town. I thrived in my new church family and loved serving others. I was sure that in the process of developing these godly relationships and helping shape young lives, I was pleasing God and growing as a person of faith.

Life was busy though. I often worked ten-hour days at the newspaper covering murder trials and other court-related issues. My husband and I soon purchased our first home, and when I wasn't working, I enjoyed decorating and trying my hand at gardening. (Let's just say my thumb isn't green.) We had great friends to spend time with, and since we had no children at that time, we often traveled on the weekends.

Usually we made it home in time for Sunday service though. My husband sang in several choirs and needed to be there, and I simply loved being in church. I appreciated hearing sermons that reminded me of God's goodness and renewed my determination to live for him. I was inspired to see others dedicate themselves to God for the first time or decide to renew their commitment because of the light they had begun to witness in other Christians' lives.

Like most twenty-somethings, I was eager to stay on the go, which meant I rarely studied the Bible outside of church. I often was too busy to sit and meditate on God's Word, other than when I prepared my lessons for my Sunday school students, whom I was trying to teach to listen for God to speak to them in contemporary ways.

Despite all that I was doing to serve God and despite the joy I felt as I did so, at some point I began to feel overwhelmed. I grew weary in trying to keep up with my schedule, both at home and at work. I eventually realized that I lacked something critical: the time to be still, to be quiet.

Rather than deciding to create that space, which would

have required me to cut back on some of my commitments, I dismissed my feelings and kept moving forward. What kind of Christian would I be to say no to a request to serve on a church committee? How could I resign from a Sunday school leadership position and say that I was honoring God?

Slowly but surely, I began to realize that I needed time to reflect on all that I was receiving from the Sunday sermons and from the lessons I was preparing for my Sunday school students so I could determine whether God had something specific to say to me. I grasped the meaning of the lessons, but I knew I hadn't left enough time in my schedule to consider how God wanted me to act on all that I was learning and teaching.

After much prayer and trepidation, I gradually pulled back from some of my church commitments — not all, but just a few, and even that felt awkward. Slowly but surely, my less-hectic pace gave me the motivation and the opportunity to nurture my friendship with God. I became familiar with how and when he was speaking specifically to me, in a language of affection created just for me. In Jeremiah 33:3 God declares, "Call to me and I will answer you and tell you great and unsearchable things you do not know." The more time I took to know him and to let the words of truth found in biblical Scriptures resonate throughout every area of my life, the more the truth of this particular verse became evident to me.

We "babes in Christ" learn to follow God's lead in stages, by taking beginner steps that lead us deeper into firsthand knowledge of him. Then we must dwell there to get acquainted with who he wants us to be. It's crucial that we walk before we run, so that when we run the race of faith both for ourselves and as God's ambassadors, we don't grow weary or lose touch with the Creator.

In my early adulthood, I thought living by the "thou shalt nots" in the Ten Commandments was the answer to salvation. As I've matured and experienced life's highs and lows without being abandoned by God, I'm continually reminded that "the earth is the Lord's, and everything in it," and that it is mine to be explored and appreciated, because God created it for all of his children, of which I am one (1 Cor. 10:26). That means we can walk this journey of faith hand in hand with God, with joy and an open heart, trusting that as we listen for his instructions and obey him when he speaks, he'll tell us when to run, and where.

Esther must have longed for God to speak when the man who had raised her, her uncle Mordecai, came to her and insisted that she approach the king and save the Jews. Esther knew what had happened to the queen who preceded her. Vashti had made the king angry and lost her head. Esther wasn't willing to walk smack dab into a similar fate. But when Mordecai warned her that she might face death anyway if she didn't try to save her people, she did what her uncle had trained her to do. She instructed Mordecai and every Jew in the city to fast and pray on her behalf. She too turned to God in prayer and fasted with her maids for three days.

Notice that after this period of dwelling with the Lord, Esther didn't rise and immediately approach the king. God seems to have instructed her how best to soften the king's heart. Esther made herself as beautiful as she could, then she went to the king's court and prayed that he would extend his golden scepter, giving her permission to approach him. When her request was granted, she certainly must have knelt in prayer again, asking God for the words to speak and the courage to follow through with a task that seemed dangerous and ill-advised.

In Esther 4:16, she declares, "If I perish, I perish." Yet think about it. Do these sound like the words of a woman who has rashly decided to honor her uncle's pleas? Unlike my young adult practice of primarily following the best earthly advice I could find, Esther took her uncle's words to heart while also turning to God for wisdom on what to do next. Realizing she had to honor Mordecai's request because the fate of her people was in her hands, Esther seemed to trust that if God was directing her down this path, he would grant her favor or bring her into his kingdom.

Put yourself in her place. What would you have done?

Esther had to run this race before she felt ready, finally understanding that maybe, just maybe, God had placed her in this role for this very reason. She was going to run with him holding her hand all the way.

Whatever stage of the race you're in, slow down enough to see if God is ready to give you direction and move you into your purpose. Don't rush the process; his timing is perfect. (Remember the story of the map I sometimes envision. God sees all and knows all long before you know how and what will unfold for you.)

If you are sprinting in your faith-walk instead of pacing

yourself, maybe it's time to slow down and wait for God to speak. If you're jogging, maintain your steady pace but know that only when you're paying attention will you see and hear what God has to say to you. If you're walking, be patient. God is grooming you for your season and your time.

Babies survive on milk until their digestive systems are mature enough to handle soft food, and eventually solids. Our efforts to know and hear from God are similar: we begin with simple, gentle instruction and eventually grow into a more mature relationship. The longer we study his teachings and dwell in his presence, the better we are able to understand and handle all he wants to reveal to us. In my own journey, I've seen how the more I've trusted him and spent time with him, the more comfortable I am with him, and the freer I feel to be me—not perfect, nor holier than thou, just me.

I've begun to recognize his sense of humor, his compassion, and even his laid-back lack of worry. Picture Jesus on the sailboat with his disciples, raising his head as he awakens from a nap and gestures for them to settle down during a storm: "Relax!" he urges them. "I've got this!" Picture him telling *you* this when worry or frustration threaten to overwhelm you. You may have heard the phrase, "Since God is up taking care of the world, we might as well get some sleep or at least calm down."

The more familiar you become with God, the more you'll find yourself wanting to be like him. Even when he's not consciously on your mind, he'll begin to influence your actions. You'll find yourself reciting Scriptures or humming the melodies of songs that praise him, and God's love and integrity will begin to show through your words and actions—regardless of whether you explicitly utter his name. The temptations that once held you captive will start to lose their power in the face of your will to obey God. There will just be something different about you that people may not be able to put their finger on. You'll know then that you have moved from being an infant in the faith and taking baby steps to walking tall in God's authority.

Keep delving into the Bible and applying its instructions to your life, your circumstances, and your relationships. Before you know it, you'll be sprinting into a level of confidence (also known as faith) that you've never before experienced. You'll not only be calling God "Father," but also "friend" and "helper."

The salvation and safety God provides is an ever-present reminder that nothing can trump him, not even a genie in a bottle. The God we develop a relationship with will stretch his arms and catch us if we stumble. He will fill a bottle with our tears and comfort us when we grieve or face rejection (Ps. 56:8). He will rejoice with us when we triumph and tiptoe alongside us as we advance from a walk to a trot to a sprint. We may not always feel his presence, but the truths in his Word assure us that he's there, every step of the way.

Scripture

John 10:3–4: The watchman opens the gate for him, and the sheep listen to his voice. He calls his own sheep by name and leads them out. When he has brought out

*all his own, he goes on ahead of them, and his sheep
follow him because they know his voice.*

Learning to Listen

Purchase a journal in which you can write down Scriptures,
notes, and questions when you study the Bible or read a
devotional book. Pull out your calendar and schedule fifteen to sixty minutes at least three days a week to spend
time getting better acquainted with God through prayer
and study. Find a version of the Bible or a devotional you
can comfortably read during your quiet time. Two of my
personal favorites are Henry Blackaby's *Experiencing God
Day by Day* and Stormie Omartian's *The Power of a Praying
Woman*. To make this time with God a constant part of
your regular routine, be sure to choose a guide that reso-
nates with you. If you settle on a devotional, still keep a
Bible handy so you can refer often to the Scriptures, to gain
context and greater understanding of what you've studied.
Jot down particular insights, comment on how what you've
read relates to your life, or note the questions you now have
after reading. Be sure to follow up on those questions at
some point in the near future, during a Bible study session
or one-on-one with a minister or Bible teacher. Remember,
questions are just as important as answers. Also, look for
signs of growth or lack of growth (behavior that you are
having difficulty changing), and write down that information in your journal too. Ask God to help you change in
ways that please him.

3

When "Perfect"
Is a Bad Word

For the first time ever, I'll publicly admit what close friends and family have known for years: I'm a recovering perfectionist. I'm fine with sharing this with you and the rest of the world because well into efforts to reform myself, I realized that while I was sometimes sidetracked by the "perfection demon," my initial intent actually had been to pursue excellence.

Chasing perfection is akin to changing dance partners halfway through a competition and still expecting to win first place. The steps you practiced with your first partner don't flow as well with someone new. The new partner doesn't move with the same rhythm or appreciate the fancy footwork your previous partner insisted you master. Still, you're expected to nail the dance on the first try and make it even stronger on the second. Excellence, on the other hand, can be viewed as a desire to perform a task well and to honor God as your motive for doing your best.

I recognized that distinction soon after my first child

was born. I marveled at how much I loved her with no strings attached, and I was filled with a new understanding of what it meant to be adored by God. He loved me in the same way I loved my firstborn, just much, much more. Knowing that kind of affection was available, and in fact already present in my life, led me to do an about-face.

I settled into my skin and relaxed more often when the mood struck me, without feeling pressured to perform to fit in. I stopped beating myself up when I made decisions or choices that I later questioned or regretted, and realized that most mistakes give us opportunities to learn and to do better the next time around. I rested in the fact that just because I existed, I was loved. Not because I was perfect, but because I was God's creation. When I looked into my daughter's innocent and trusting eyes and received one of her toothless grins, my heart melted. Long before she could say "mommy" or ask for a hug or kiss, I wanted to give all of myself to her and show her in as many ways as possible how much I loved her.

The realization that even the deep affection I had for this child was nowhere near the adoration Christ had for me when he formed me in my mother's womb touched me deeply. He knew I would be born and not have a clue about him; he knew that I would mess up, and that when I was taught about him, I sometimes would be too busy to give him my full attention. Still, he loved me. Not only did he love me; he sought me out and nurtured my growth, just as I was doing with my daughter.

I thought about how I would feel if someday she grew

too busy to accept my hugs or take my calls. I'd be hurt and sad, but it wouldn't stop me from loving her. Those musings helped me understand how God must feel when we neglect him or take him for granted. He loves us dearly, but our relationship isn't all that it could be.

It's crucial for a woman longing to be closer to God to be aware of the fine line between being the best for the sake of garnering praise and respect from others and aiming to be the best to bring God glory. This very issue caused friction between Martha and Mary, two sisters who befriended and loved Jesus in biblical times. The story is told in Luke 10:38–42:

> As Jesus and his disciples were on their way, he came to a village where a woman named Martha opened her home to him. She had a sister called Mary, who sat at the Lord's feet listening to what he said. But Martha was distracted by all the preparations that had to be made. She came to him and asked, "Lord, don't you care that my sister has left me to do the work by myself? Tell her to help me!"
>
> "Martha, Martha," the Lord answered, "you are worried and upset about many things, but only one thing is needed. Mary has chosen what is better, and it will not be taken away from her."

Neither sister was wrong, but in her effort to have everything "just so" for Jesus, Martha in effect missed out on some precious quality time with Jesus. When she complained about her sister's laziness, Jesus told her that she too should have been relaxing at his feet and getting to know him better.

I've been there. I want my floors to shine, my sink to sparkle, and my bathrooms spotless when guests arrive, or else I'm not quite comfortable that they're comfortable. My eldest sister, on the other hand, believes that one shouldn't fret about cleaning so thoroughly until the guests are gone. Her philosophy? They're there to live and spend time with their hosts, so why get everything tidied up just to be mussed over again anyway? She's relaxed when company comes, while I can be frenzied. I think the true balance lies between the two, so that neither of us miss a visit from the Master nor forsake a chance to experience the love and wisdom he's seeking to speak into our lives.

Perfection is limiting because it inhibits your ability to be sensitive to others, and thus distances you from them. If you seem so good and so "put together" at all times, people struggle to see God's compassion. The fabulous side of him, through which he has crowned you with glory, may be evident, but the loving side of him, through which he has healed your broken heart or saved your life when everyone around you was preparing to unplug life support, remains veiled.

It is in your seasons of brokenness that God can use you best. People pinpoint your flaws and wonder how you still manage to thrive. They watch you smile through the tears and question from where you could possibly be finding joy. They see you stumble, but get back up again and dust yourself off with a chuckle, squaring your shoulders to indicate that you may have lost a battle, but the war is still yours to win.

Perfection seeks to mask the contradictions of life, because perfection is all about fear—hiding the real you. It seeks to cover up the pain you've felt from rejection or to mask the insecurities that have plagued you because you fear that you are inadequate for some reason—your weight, lack of education, or a million other reasons.

Shon Gables, anchor of the nationally syndicated television talk show *Black Enterprise Business Report* and a former anchor with the CBS flagship news station in New York City, can attest to this. Shon is a lovely and talented broadcast reporter and self-professed recovering workaholic. As a single mother to her first son, she worked ten- to fourteen-hour days learning the broadcast news business and paying her dues. That pace required her to leave her son in the care of nannies and tutors who helped her juggle it all. When she remarried and had a second child, she lived in the house of her dreams, and her career as a television morning news anchor flourished.

Yet her marriage began to crumble as did her perfect world along with it. Soon, she was out of work and struggling to care for her sons as a single mom again. She realized this time around that the key to her success wouldn't lie in landing another high-pressure, high-powered job; she needed to trust God to provide.

Shon asked God to bless her with an anchor position that would give her the time and flexibility to raise her sons herself and be home with them on a regular basis. She asked him to forgive her for her mistakes and to give her the courage to apologize to her former husbands and anyone else she may have hurt.

Then she began to write the vision she wanted for her life. It did not include perfection; instead, it resonated with dreams and goals that gave her space and time for a thriving relationship with God and her family and for meaningful experiences in her career as a reporter. "One wonders, 'God is this all there is?'" Shon admits. "Until I finally became resolute that I would thank God in good, bad, and even weary seasons."

As she listens for God's direction, she is learning to trust, to rest, and to wait with open ears and an open heart. She is focused on raising her sons with faith and wisdom. From Shon's perspective—and mine—that level of sweet surrender trumps anything perfection would have yielded.

When you talk to God and tell him you're tired of trying to be perfect, he'll stroke your cheek with the whisper of a wind that signals his tender questions: "What took you so long to approach me? Are you ready to try it my way?"

God's way is risky because it requires surrender and vulnerability from you. It calls for a diminished focus on your image and a heightened concentration on the state of your heart. There's no need to book an appearance on Oprah to tell the world all your problems or publicly shed your tears. You must simply begin shifting your attention toward honoring God, who is the only perfect one, and in the process, strive with all your heart to serve him well.

Over time, your tense shoulders will drop. You'll invite

guests over even though there are still dishes in the sink. You'll grow comfortable being you and learn to laugh at your mishaps and mistakes. You'll find the strength to shed your mask and give up the superwoman title, replacing it with a "God knows I did the best that I could at the time" attitude.

When you reach that point, it won't feel like much of a struggle. Instead, it will feel like you're finally living.

Learning to Listen

Decide today to stop pursuing perfection and instead seek a relationship with God that brings you peace and gives him glory. When you make this change, you'll find that the more you let your guard down, the more the Lord is filling those empty or insecure spaces. His presence will cause you to operate in excellence instead of pursuing perfection.

Meditate on these two verses for a week, and at the end of that period, detail in writing how you will apply them to your personal situation.

John 10:10: "The thief comes only to steal and kill and destroy; I have come that they may have life, and have it to the full."

Colossians 3:23: "Whatever you do, work at it with all your heart, as working for the Lord, not for men."

As I meditated on Colossians 3:23, I decided that I would always strive to write and speak about issues that have meaning and uplift readers rather than subjects that merely yield income. That means you won't find me penning erotic novels, despite the fact that they sell well, or crafting articles for the *National Enquirer* or *Star* magazine, unless those tabloids decide to drastically shift their focus and concentrate on what is good and spirit-filled and published to draw readers toward healthier relationships with each other and Christ.

When I meditated on John 10:10, I decided that when I feel pressure to be perfect or seem to be having one of the "terrible, horrible, no good very bad days" Judith Viorst describes in one of her *Alexander*-series children's books, instead of giving in to the frustration, I will remember that God works everything out for my good and that this too shall pass.

Study and pray over these two verses at the beginning of each day during the week, before you launch into the tasks filling your to-do list or calendar. Let the Scriptures guide your thoughts and your actions. When you sit down and apply them to your circumstances, consider how these passages can help you surrender the "perfection demon" that may be hounding you. Then ask God for deliverance.

4

Letting Go of the Life You Imagined

In most communities across America, when people greet someone new, among the first questions they ask are "What do you do?" and/or "Where do you live?"

It's sad that in our "melting pot" nation we continue to judge each other's worth by our looks, our zip codes, our titles, our marital status, or our ancestry. If you live in centers of political and financial power like Washington, DC and New York City, this is likely prevalent. Status is an issue everywhere though, even in rural communities and urban neighborhoods where residents are struggling to survive.

For some of us, being able to answer these questions with the "right" answers keeps us thriving. But what happens if you can no longer check off all the impressive boxes? The economic woes our nation has faced in recent times have forced many families out of their homes in the elite zip codes, left thousands out of work, and caused a mass return to a much simpler lifestyle than we've seen in this generation.

Wherever you find yourself today in regard to the fallout

from the economy, now is a good time to embrace the message in Isaiah 40:8 that reminds us everything will fade away except the Word of God. Standing on God's promises means we no longer have to rely on the status the world gives us. When we can let go of worrying about how we are perceived by others and whether we'll fit into a certain social group, we're ready to hear God speak.

Polly Chamberlain realized that nearly a decade ago when she relocated from a middle-class Maryland suburb to start over in urban Richmond, Virginia. A pretty and petite forty-something mother of two who had once been a stay-at-home mom, she found herself divorced and searching for meaning.

Polly decided early on that her life in Richmond wasn't going to mirror the publicly perfect facade she had maintained for almost twenty years. Instead, she wanted to live authentically (flaws and all), do work she could be proud of, and make a difference.

She capitalized on her training as a medical transcriptionist to find a job, and in her spare time she volunteered at a church in downtown Richmond that served a free lunchtime meal to anyone who stopped by. Many of the people who lined up before noon and strolled through the meal line were homeless or clearly living on society's fringes.

Polly filled their plates with heaping spoonfuls of whatever particular dish she had been assigned to serve that day and greeted the meal guests with hellos and blessings. But she felt uneasy, as if she should be doing more. She asked God to show her what was missing, and he brought to mind the passage of Scripture that described Jesus' last few hours with his disciples. Jesus washed their feet to express his love and to show that his entire existence on earth had been to serve them and to teach them to serve others:

> *When he had finished washing their feet, he put on his clothes and returned to his place. "Do you understand what I have done for you?" he asked them. "You call me 'Teacher' and 'Lord,' and rightly so, for that is what I am. Now that I, your Lord and Teacher, have washed your feet, you also should wash one another's feet. I have set you an example that you should do as I have done for you."*

John 13:12–15

Polly's minister recited that same passage in a sermon soon after she had begun wrestling with how to move forward, and within days, she developed a new habit: she started noticing the ragged and worn shoes the men and women wore when they showed up for the church's Friday meal.

That triggered memories of her days as a youth Sunday school teacher in Maryland. She recalled a foot washing ritual she had performed one year for her teenage students as part of a ceremony on service. She remembered how intimate and giving the exercise had been and wrestled with whether God was asking her to somehow offer the same gift to the strangers she encountered on Fridays.

Polly kept praying until she felt a sense of urgency to know these men and women's stories and how they had come to their particular places in life. She met with her pastor and asked if she could start a ministry that would give her more time to interact with them during lunchtime.

A few weeks later, she set up shop in a corner of the church's cafeteria where she slipped on plastic gloves, filled a bucket with warm water, and washed the cracked, blistered, and sometimes sore-covered feet of men and women who had only been expecting a meal.

Polly didn't just soothe their feet; she talked to them as she washed and got to know them. She asked about their health and sometimes their families. They asked about hers and began to see her as a friend. Each week they sought her out. This was their pampering time and her few hours of personal ministry.

Polly prayed while she worked. Maybe hearing about their experiences and concerns as she cleaned and pampered their feet would help her understand them. Maybe she would stop making assumptions about how and why they had landed in a challenging situation. As she slipped their freshly washed soles into a new pair of white cotton socks, maybe she could encourage them and pray for them if they wanted.

The Polly Chamberlain who washed these feet wasn't the same woman who had been a churchgoing volunteer who sometimes prejudged the panhandlers and homeless adults she encountered on Maryland's streets. She had triumphed over a challenging time in her life and had learned to hear God speaking to her heart. In listening to him, she was evolving into the woman he had destined her to be.

Polly had only washed feet once before and that effort

had focused on kids she loved. In humbling herself to serve in a new and unanticipated way, she found the freedom to let go of who she thought she was and embrace who God was calling her to be.

Since starting that ministry in 2004, Polly has watched it grow to include other volunteers from the church, and she has witnessed her own growth. Her life is much fuller than it would have been if she had not listened to God. He transformed her heart, led her to a purpose that touches those who are considered "the least of these," and in the process, gave her a chance to act as God's heart and hands on earth.

God isn't calling each of us to start a foot-washing ministry, but when you begin to quiet yourself and let go of your agenda or your plans for your life, he'll show you where and how he wants you to serve. This doesn't mean you cancel your plans to attend the college of your dreams or stop pursuing the promotion at work you've been lobbying for. It means that as you work to achieve these goals, you talk to God throughout the process and ask him to give you wisdom and to close any doors you shouldn't walk through.

Just as he made Polly uncomfortable with simply serving up a dish of much-appreciated food, he'll nudge your spirit when he's ready to use you for a specific purpose. But like Polly's, your heart has to be open. You can't be distracted or afraid. You have to walk toward his calling.

In the Old Testament book of Judges, Deborah found herself in this position when she served as the only female judge of Israel (a position of leadership before there were kings) and became the first female military leader in biblical times. Old Testament accounts of her service describe how as a prophet she sought out God and listened when he spoke. She delivered a message from the Lord to a warrior named Barak, informing him that God wanted him to form an army of ten thousand and go to battle against the people of Canaan (Judg. 4:6–7).

The Bible doesn't spell this out, but it was evident from Barak's response that he respected Deborah's relationship with and communication with God. He refused to go to war without her at his side. Deborah fearlessly led the men into battle on behalf of the Lord and helped achieve a victory for the Israelites that allowed them to live in peace for forty years.

I doubt that Deborah dreamed as a child of being a military leader or even a judge. It was out of character for the role women played during biblical days. Yet when God called her to action, she didn't hesitate or question whether she was to go. She must have had a knowing, an innate feeling, that since this task had fallen to her, God was nudging her to follow through.

When we say we're ready to hear from God, we're required to back up our words with actions. I have to let go of the Stacy I want to be, or the Stacy I think I already am, in order to become a woman after God's heart. I have to humble myself enough to be used by him, even when I'm tired, doubtful, or frustrated, or have plans of my own that would lead me down a different path. Whenever I follow God's lead, I'm always blessed by how he alters my just-good-enough offerings into abundant blessings for others.

I remember longing to write about women's health for one of the newspapers for which I worked. I'd had an interest in this topic for a while, and when the veteran reporter who covered this issue moved on, I interviewed for the job armed with confidence and a portfolio filled with story ideas and creative possibilities. I was crushed when the position went to another writer who was just as qualified, if not more, than me.

What landed in my lap instead was an opportunity to write about social issues. I had also developed a loose interest in family issues and, in fact, had begun to pursue a graduate degree in sociology at a local university. That alone should have told me God was orchestrating something awesome. I was given the social issues position at the height of welfare reform in Virginia and across the nation, and I hit the ground running with a series of stories that changed not only the lives of the people I profiled as they worked their way off of public assistance, but also readers who now had a different perspective on the eight women and one man (a single father) who had sought the aid. I wound up covering issues on the social issues beat that allowed me to put a face on everything from domestic violence and child health insurance to small nonprofit agencies that, for the longest time, had gone unnoticed. The work on this beat led to my being offered a newspaper column, and eventually, some of the subjects I wrote about as a reporter served as a foundation for some of the themes that worked their way into my novels. Who knew? God, of course. In letting go of my disappointment over the position I thought I wanted and embracing what was offered instead, I found myself being given a source for book material and for professional relationships that I still find relevant today.

As you think about areas of your life where things may not have turned out as you had hoped or planned, and you've found yourself way off course, comfort yourself with the certainty that wherever you are, you are still in God's presence. Wherever you are, he can speak to you. You may not have the education, money, or support from family and friends to pursue the dream you've long wanted to make your reality, but talk to God about it. If there's a particular project or matter he's calling you to tackle, he will open doors on your behalf. We can make excuse after excuse about why something is impossible or why it won't work, but when we do that, we're disregarding the truths of the Bible, which declares that with God, all things are possible (Matt. 19:26).

God knows your limitations better than you, but remember the map I described earlier in the book — the one that serves as a metaphor for the all-knowing perspective God possesses? He sees your current situation and what he's calling you to do, and the resources that you need are already on the way. In some instances, they have to be activated by your faith and by taking the first step toward action.

Deborah didn't just deliver God's message to Barak and return to her judge's seat under the palm tree. She agreed to go to battle with him, to see through to the end the instruction God had given her.

This doesn't mean you decide on a whim to follow a long-held passion or dream and declare God's blessing over it. Rather, you must find the courage to listen to what he's already speaking to your heart and knock on the doors that you feel him nudging you to walk through.

For example, attend a small business seminar or enroll in a class at a local college that can give you the skills or knowledge to move your dream closer to reality. Find a trusted friend or neighbor to swap babysitting with so you can schedule small chunks of time to pursue your goals. Carve out some quiet time to sit with yourself and be honest about who or what might be holding you back and what you can change about the situation. Ask God to lead you to spiritual mentors who can pray with you and help you determine whether the path you want to set out on is indeed a calling from God and not of your own making.

As you read the Bible more regularly and spend more time in prayer, you can begin letting go of the "you" you think you're supposed to be. When you draw closer to him, you'll find yourself more able to surrender to God's will without getting stuck.

Apart from his guidance, it's easy to remain in spiritual limbo — where we think we hear God directing us to do something but since we aren't sure, we sit and wait. Or, we keep pushing forward instead of slowing down to clearly hear what he is directing us to do. If you find yourself in either of these positions, that may mean you haven't really let go. You've told God you're ready and you've asked him to provide answers, but when the answers surfaced and they weren't what you expected or wanted, you took back your limited control. You're not alone — I've been there too.

But what if Polly had squirmed at the idea of washing the feet of men and women who walked the streets for hours at a time and mostly had no place to call home? What if I had refused to take the social issues beat and instead continued to cover courts long after the job had become comfortable and routine?

What if the biblical warrior Deborah had said she wasn't up to the task? Or what if the Moabite woman in the book of Ruth had decided after the death of her husband to abandon her mother-in-law Naomi and return to her native land? Instead, Ruth professed her love and loyalty to Naomi and toiled in the fields to provide for herself and the older woman. Ruth had no way of knowing that by embracing the life she had been given rather than pursuing one of her own making, she would be anything other than a struggling widow. Because she let go of what appeared to be best for her, God blessed her with a second husband, Boaz, and she birthed a son Obed, who was the grandfather of King David, of the lineage of Jesus Christ.

Letting go of your vision for your life doesn't mean you don't have a vision at all. (I still have goals and dreams that I'm asking God to bring to life.) It means that we end each prayer about our vision with the words "Thy will be done." It means that after we have prayed, we don't rise from our knees or lift our heads just yet. We sit in silence and let the silence permeate our being, in case Jesus wants to speak right then and there. It means that when our path is directed to what might seem like left field, if we feel the tugging of the Holy Spirit to follow, we do. If we feel uneasy, we stop and pray and ask God for divine wisdom.

God will be with us and answer us in our times of need. That's why it's so important to be connected to him. When we move ourselves out of the way, and act in faith, it's possible to trust that when we push one door and it remains closed, then push the next and it only cracks open, the third door that we walk through will somehow draw us closer to God and to his purpose for our lives. God's track record is excellent. We can trust him with our whole hearts, and he will honor that love and devotion with victories we never could have imagined. His results can make the plans we had envisioned for ourselves seem like child's play.

Prayer

Dear Father, please fill me with your Holy Spirit and give me a heart like yours. Help me surrender my will to yours. Give me a passion for what you're directing me to do, or make me uncomfortable if need be, to move me where you want me to be. Help me trust you throughout this process and move forward in faith. Most importantly, help me recognize when you are speaking and give me the courage to let go of my vision and embrace yours. Amen.

Pray this prayer every day for a week and decide that your only ambition during this period will be for your heart to desire the plans God has for your life. Don't stay stuck as you're waiting to "hear" from God. As is explained in James 2:20–24, faith without works is dead. Move as you feel led by God, and if you still aren't sure whether it's the right path, trust that he will give you peace when you begin to operate inside his will and at his direction.

part 2

Learning to Listen

I sat in an audiologist's office a few years ago and reviewed a report with her that proved my husband and children had been right: something was wrong with my hearing. It wasn't natural to miss the ringing of our doorbell, fail to hear my son or daughter when they called to me from another part of the house, or have the volume on the TV turned up so loud when I watched a show. They had been urging me for months to get checked.

I finally relented when the truth smacked me in the face. I was preparing to launch a new book and would be speaking at the church we attended during both morning services about the themes of faith, forgiveness, and transformation in this new novel. I sat in an alcove to the side of the sanctuary so I would have ready access to the pulpit when the pastor called me. However, both times he gave me a rousing introduction and asked me to join him, I didn't move. The friend and church member sitting next to me had to nudge me and tell me to hurry to the platform.

That rattled me. How could I not hear when he had beckoned me through the microphone and his booming voice had clearly permeated the speakers? The audiologist explained on that November morning that I had a condition that was causing the bones in my ears to fuse together, preventing me from hearing low-toned sounds, such as my pastor's deep baritone voice.

The situation wasn't dire. I could still hear people right in front of me or even across the room as long as they enunciated and there wasn't other interference. But more and more often I had found myself asking audience members at speaking engagements to repeat questions, and I still had to have the TV volume fairly high to get the gist of the plot or details of the news story unfolding before me.

Like many of us do when we want to avoid a situation or deal with it later, I convinced myself that the hearing aid the audiologist recommended was just an excuse to lighten my bank account. She, on the other hand, insisted that it was about quality of life: Why go through my daily routines straining to hear, or missing pieces of conversations or directives, when I didn't have to?

Several months later, when I finally accepted her advice, I realized she was right. I may not have been deaf and unable to communicate with others, but after I tucked the tiny, nearly invisible hearing aid into one of my ears and gave it a few seconds to turn on, I was stunned. What a relief it was to watch a show or listen to a sermon or speech and not fret about the one or two words that escaped me every few minutes, leading me to guess at the context of a conversation. What a joy to know that I could hear the doorbell, and my children, and the sound of rain on my roof.

Learning to listen to God can be a similar life-improving experience. The cliché is right on target: we don't know what we're missing until we try it. Once I adopted the habit of talking to God throughout the day about every decision or issue I faced, I grew more comfortable with waiting for his responses.

I find it hard to remember a time when I didn't call God "Daddy" or tell him exactly how I was feeling, even when it wasn't pretty. I know he's always listening and imagine him sometimes shaking his head at me, especially on those days when I'm asking forgiveness again and again. The crucial next step is for me to then be silent and let him answer however he sees fit.

Prior to the incident at my church, I had been praying about whether I needed that hearing aid, and that Sunday morning when I realized important sounds were escaping me, I could no longer say I was unsure. God doesn't always speak so literally, but that's what makes listening an art. Most of us consider ourselves good listeners. We may look directly at the person who is speaking to us, end a phone call, or show our attentiveness in some other way, but unless we focus on the way they utter the words or peer into their eyes, we may not fully grasp what they're saying.

When Jesus spoke, his disciples often misinterpreted or dismissed the significance of his message. When he declared, "I will be with you always," they likely sighed with relief and took that to mean that he'd always be their "ride or die" buddy, leading them from town to town to offer salvation to the multitudes.

Maybe they weren't ready to hear what he was really saying: "ride or die" meant that death would come into the picture. He would have to leave earth in order to fulfill his Father's will and provide salvation to mankind forever. He was promising that his spirit would always linger. John, James, Peter, Andrew, and the others didn't pick up on that. They may have heard him, but clearly they weren't listening.

We are much the same way. We hear what we want to hear, especially if it's a yes we're waiting for or the approval to move forward with a desire or wish. The hesitant voice in which the agreement is offered from other people, or maybe even the frown, is ignored. All we've heard is "go forth," or "all is well," missing the silent "but" or warning of "at your own risk."

When we're straining to hear from God we'll read a verse in a particular book of the Bible but not review the entire chapter to understand the full context of that one sentence. We'll pray and sense that God is telling us to take a stance, but refuse to wait for him to direct us on the best methods to accomplish his will.

Listening requires something most of us are in short supply of—patience and discipline. Because we live in such a technologically advanced world that equips us with faster computers, news at our fingertips and on our cell phones, and the ability to connect online in seconds with people on the other side of the world, patience and self-control can seem like punishment. In our drive-thru window society, where we can easily super size a meal or pay for body parts that make us feel whole, discipline and sacrifice for the sake of hearing God more clearly are in short supply too.

Listening for the heart of God and then acting upon his direction is the hallmark of miracles. The woman at the well listened 'to Jesus' offer to quench her thirst but heard his deeper message — a chance to receive a life-altering drink from the well of life. As it was for her, such a drink can be the beginning of our spiritual transformation and a life that can be used to God's glory in history-making ways.

5

Embracing Silence

During the summer before my senior year in college, I landed an internship at a newspaper in Albuquerque, New Mexico—about as far from my conservative Arkansas roots as a sheltered homebody could get. The first thing I decided the day after I arrived and peered out a window at the mountains looming over the city was that Albuquerque was absolutely beautiful. That revelation was followed by an ache for the familiarity of home that left me feeling like a foreigner in a land I wasn't sure I was ready to explore.

Fortunately, I shared a rental house with two women about ten years older than me who were energetic and eager to enjoy all that Albuquerque had to offer. They introduced me to their friends and helped me navigate my way around the city.

One of the ladies, Pam, was a fellow writer at the local newspaper. One weekend, she invited me to accompany her to a monastery nestled in the mountains north of Santa Fe. "Sure," I said, eager to get away for the weekend since I had no other plans.

I was twenty-one and used to having access to life's

modern conveniences. I had no idea what I was getting myself into. After a brief stop in Abiquiu, where we visited the home and studio of renowned artist Georgia O'Keefe, we chugged up the mountainside in Pam's older-model car, pushing it to the limits and admiring the fact that anyone would make the effort to locate and book a stay at this mountainside retreat. Pam was writing a feature story about the place for Albuquerque's afternoon newspaper (which has since folded).

When we reached our destination and I was escorted to a modest, clean cabin that would serve as my home-away-from-home for the weekend, I felt like I had stepped back in time, to the days of Laura Ingalls Wilder. This wasn't the Midwest plains described in the *Little House on the Prairie* series of novels, but the stripped-down room with nothing more than a bed, a sink, and a lantern reminded me of the scenes I'd read in her books and viewed on the namesake television series. There was no electricity, running water, or telephone service. I thought I might die.

Pam, my Albuquerque roommate, had a separate room, which she seemed eager to retreat to for the evening. Before darkness fell, however, the two of us sat on a ledge and peered over the mountain across the vast wilderness that stretched before us. There was a stillness I had never before experienced. Pam thought it was beautiful and calming — perfect for reflection and recovery. I, on the other hand, found myself jittery. Within five minutes of sitting in silence I was itching for a book to read, some music to soothe my ears, or ... *something*. Anything.

The quietness was the monastery's key attraction, though. Pam and I met men and women who had come from different parts of the country for different reasons to be closer to God and to hear where he might be leading them next. The monks served a simple breakfast and lunch during which we could not talk.

When we did strike up brief conversations with other guests, it was in the required whispers, as if speaking in elevated voices might disturb God. We had been told that because the monastery sat in a canyon, sound traveled easily and could be heard by guests in their rooms.

On Sunday morning, nearly twenty-four hours into our stay, the monks led a worship service filled with chanting, biblical readings, and group singing unaccompanied by music. People from nearby towns traveled up the mountain for the service and told Pam they came occasionally because the beauty of the place and the complete focus on God reminded them of what was important in life.

I questioned at the time what was wrong with me. Why wasn't I as excited as they were about this "opportunity" to commune with God? Why hadn't I been able to still my thoughts and soothe my boredom long enough to listen, just in case God had something to tell me?

I yearned to leave that eerily quiet retreat as if I were allergic to its air and dust.

When we loaded Pam's car with our bags and began our descent, I was elated. I grudgingly acknowledged that it had been a worthwhile experience, but I was thankful to be returning to civilization.

Years later, when I found myself longing for answers from God to situations or problems that left me confused or angry, I lamented the opportunity I had wasted to get alone with the Creator and seek his direction for my life. I had been too naive to appreciate the beauty of God's natural landscape and too afraid to open my heart and hear whatever God wanted to say back then. I was a know-it-all, focused on the plans I had set in motion. That mountaintop visit had been little more than an unusual weekend excursion.

I understand now that it was a golden opportunity. Imagine if I had seized it and knelt before God in that holy place to receive his anointing. Imagine if I had listened for his whisper among the trees or opened myself to his nudges through the encouragement and experiences that others there that weekend shared.

I wonder if I might have been transformed somehow. Yet, maybe I was. Whenever I reflect upon that season, I tell myself the value wasn't entirely lost, because I can look back now and realize that anytime we're given the space to get alone with God, it's not to be wasted. I understand now the value of taking time to listen and having the courage to hear him.

Maybe I wasn't ready for whatever God wanted to share with me that summer, or maybe I just *think* I wasn't ready. Can you recall ever being in a similar situation, where God was clearly providing an opportunity for the two of you to connect and you ran the other way? Or maybe, unlike me, you didn't run, and you found yourself intimately bound to God in a way you hadn't imagined possible.

Whatever your answer, the good news is that the Creator we serve is a God of second, third, fourth, and countless chances. I may have missed an awesome opportunity in New Mexico, but he didn't give up on me. He kept nudging and knocking until finally I said, "Here I am, Lord. Speak to me."

You too can make that declaration to God. Don't worry about your youth or your age or your bad habits or your half-done tasks. Just ask God to embrace you where you are today and to give you a new chance to commit your life to him.

Even if you are afraid, tell him you're ready to listen. Ask him to hold your hand and show you it won't hurt. If anything, he wants to speak to the hurts you're already experiencing and give you comfort. With just one whisper, he can ease your fears and prove that walking with him is much better than any other mode of travel.

Learning to Listen

Think about the times when God might have been ready and willing to speak to you and you hesitated. Write about that experience or those experiences in your journal and explain why you think you avoided listening. Then write down what you would have wanted to hear if you had been brave enough to listen.

If you've never had an experience like this, where you remember God trying to strike up a conversation with you, imagine what you would have done had you been at that monastery I've described. Would you have been anxious to leave or eager to dwell in his presence? What would you have wanted to hear from God?

Over the next few days, review what you've written in answer to these questions and talk to God about it. Apologize for being afraid and admit if you still find it hard to open up to him. Then ask him to give you the peace, the patience, and the discipline to listen.

6

Appreciate Your Baby Steps

By the time I was thirty and the mother of one, I looked back on that summer in Albuquerque wistfully, choosing to remember the beauty of the place and the people who embraced me rather than dwell on the times I wasted longing to return to familiar surroundings.

At this point in my life I had begun trying to resume my childhood passion: writing fiction. Then I learned that baby number two was on the way. I was elated, and preparing for his arrival consumed my focus and energy. We learned that he was a boy at the routine five-month checkup and that all was progressing well. I became addicted to HDTV and learned how best to decoupage and paint the walls of his room. I prepared my toddler daughter to become a big sister. I ate properly and gave up caffeine for the sake of his health.

So when I slipped down a single stair in my home during my eighth month of pregnancy, I thought little of it. It was just a slight bump, not a full fall. I debated whether to call my doctor, but since I had a routine checkup scheduled for a few days later, I didn't bother.

During that visit early the following week, the nurse

practitioner who saw me said all seemed well; the baby would be born in another four weeks or so and he seemed fine. Then I mentioned that I had slipped on the stairs and thought she should know. She suggested that this far into pregnancy I should have called, because anything could have happened; you just never know.

As would be the case with most pregnant moms receiving that kind of admonition, I didn't sleep well that night. I called my doctor the next day and asked for an ultrasound, just to make sure the baby was okay. My doctor readily agreed, and I returned to her office later that morning for this brief test, which I thought would put my mind at ease for the final few weeks before the baby arrived.

Instead, what should have been a routine checkup led to another series of tests. The ultrasound technician had seen something unusual on my son's heart. We were sent to a specialist who performed an ultra-sensitive ultrasound that detected a tumor in the left chamber. It could mean nothing or it could be a sign of a serious illness that would impair my son's health long term. There was no way to know until he was born.

You can imagine life at my house over the next month. I walked the halls many nights, crying out to God to spare my son this illness and fretting about what I would do if he had it. I couldn't sleep so I read Scripture after Scripture that reminded me God was a healer and that he listened to the prayers and pleas of those who served him.

I asked God to speak to me, to give me a sign that all would be well. Yet during this season when I felt like I needed God most, I felt more disconnected from him than I had in my entire life. Because I knew his Word, I knew he was walking through this terrifying experience with me. I knew that he was present during every visit I now made to the doctor twice a week. I knew that he heard my prayers and pleas for everything to work out okay.

Along with this knowledge of him, though, I wanted to hear from him. I listened in the middle of the night when I couldn't sleep. I listened during the day as I read Bible passages. The more I learned about the awful disease that my baby boy could potentially be diagnosed with, the more eager I was to hear God tell me not to weep because he was on the case.

Throughout that period I never heard him. I didn't feel his presence cloaking me and I wasn't at peace. Not because I doubted that he could or would come through, and not because I was angry or frustrated at him. He just didn't seem near.

Each passage I read in the Bible assured me that he was, though. Psalm 34:18 declared that "the Lord is close to the brokenhearted and saves those who are crushed in spirit." Isaiah 53:4 said Jesus was a healer. Psalm 34:6 said God heard my cries.

Because I couldn't feel his presence or receive a sign that he was trying to speak to me, all I could do was trust. I surrendered my heart to him along with my hopes and my fears and asked him to help me through whatever was in store. I asked him to return his presence to me and to guide me when I didn't know what to do next.

On the day our son was scheduled to be born, one of the ministers from our church joined my husband and me at the hospital and prayed for our baby to arrive healthy and whole. His birth was unusually dramatic because technicians were on hand to whisk him away to the neonatal intensive care unit if necessary, and to hook him up to machines he might need to help his heart work.

But when he was born on that sunny afternoon in late spring, they immediately allowed me to do something they said I wouldn't be able to do: hold my son and kiss him. He was then checked out and whisked away for observation, and while they confirmed that a tumor was lodged in his heart, they were pleasantly perplexed by the fact that he didn't need intensive care treatment.

His first few days of life were filled with tests and visits from specialists who sought to determine whether he was healthy enough to go home. I was a spool of tightly wound nerves, but as each doctor came to my bedside to update me on my son's status, I slowly unwound. No tumors on the brain. No tumors on the kidneys. Normal heart functioning. This baby would have to be monitored closely for the next few years, but he could go home without any special monitors and be nurtured like any other healthy infant.

My fear and nervousness didn't leave right away. I kept him nearby in a bassinet and jumped every time he cried, afraid to let him strain his heart too much for the first few weeks, despite the doctors' assurances that he was okay. Then slowly but surely I heard the whispers from God that I needed.

He guided me to the right doctors to care for my son's special needs; he gave me the strength to parent him as I would have without this medical condition; and he allowed me to relax and enjoy this lively boy's babyhood. My husband and I didn't know yet how this tumor would affect our son's health long term, but we were determined to love him and celebrate life with him.

Six months, one year, eighteen months later, every test we took revealed that the tumor was still lodged in his heart's left ventricle. Yet no other tumors had appeared in his body on other organs, and that was great news. I realized around the time of his first-birthday visit with his cardiologist what part of this experience may have been about: my learning to trust God with something (or in this case some-one) I desperately loved.

There was nothing I could do to heal this child, to take away the challenges he had to endure. No matter what I did, he needed care and attention from doctors familiar with his potential illness. All I could do was love him and rest in my belief that God would keep him safe.

I realized that was what God had wanted from me all along: the surrender of my will and desire to his, to realize that I was the honorary caretaker of his precious gift, and to understand that while my son was the focus of this trial, God could use it for my good. Out of necessity, I had learned to fully trust him.

As I dwelled in the Scriptures and reviewed God's promises, suddenly I had a renewed belief that they weren't just empty words on a page. He was showing those promises to be true in my life. He was speaking to me through the Bible since I wasn't able to hear him any other way.

As my son began to crawl and then pull himself up and attempt to walk, I understood that God had been taking me through a remarkably similar stage in terms of my faith. When I hadn't been able to hear him speaking or feel his presence, God had been nearby, weeping with me and encouraging me to stay strong and give a larger dose of faith a try. I had wanted him to cradle me and carry me through those scary days; instead he had taken a step back to extend his hands toward me, allowing me to toddle until I gained the balance and the skill to walk toward him on my own. Just as I stepped back from my son and stretched out my arms, urging him to take a step or two toward me instead of crawling, God had been doing the same to me.

He wanted me to know that regardless of whether I could feel him or whether I received a tangible sign that he was with me, his Word was always a true and steadfast guide. If I would rely on the promises there, I could be sure that he would never leave nor forsake me. As surely as I would catch my son if he stumbled in his quest to learn to walk, God was willing to catch me.

First, he wanted me to have the courage to believe in him. The more I did so, my faith grew by leaps and bounds. I began asking God to give me wisdom before I read my Bible, and when I opened it, he spoke clearly through the passages I studied.

When my son turned three, we took him to his cardiologist for his annual exam and she joyfully reported that there was good news. The tumor on my son's heart was no longer visible. As some infantile tumors do, this one had dissolved on its own. No biopsy was necessary and no further testing of my son's various organs would be needed. He was given a clean bill of health.

I weep as I share this story because I know that God granted a miracle to this little boy who had been covered in prayer and showered in love for thirty-six months. I also shed tears because I know that the other miracle occurred in me. Had we not experienced this frightening and stressful season in our lives, I don't know that my faith would have grown as much or that I would have learned to listen for God in new and unexpected ways.

He used my deep love for my son to show me his deep love for me, and how sometimes he gets our attention in ways that make us sit up and self-correct. I hadn't been wrong in pleading for God to speak to me. He just wanted me to search for him in new ways, trusting that however he spoke, his word would be good and true.

Learning to Listen

You may not be able to readily think of a miracle God has granted, or you may be struggling with a situation in which you prayed for a miracle he didn't seem to grant. Ask God to speak to your heart about a time when you have needed to hear from him and he didn't seem to respond. Ask him to reveal to you whether he did actually answer and you missed it, or to share with you why he stepped back and took his hands off of the situation. This week, think about the unusual ways God has spoken to you—in difficult seasons or at times of waiting or when you were most fearful. If you couldn't hear from him directly, what did you do to try and seek him? Consider whether God led you down that path for a reason—to teach you new ways to hear him, to draw you away from a crutch, or to encourage you to call on him more directly.

Prayer

Dear God, I don't always understand your methods. I simply want to hear from you and know what you want me to do or how I should handle a particular situation. It seems like you've left me all alone, yet your Word tells me you are very near. Lord, please show me what you want me to learn from this situation and how I can use it to grow closer to you. I can't figure it out on my own. Give me the patience to wait for your answers, and during the process, the ability to praise your holy name. Amen.

7

Unexpected Blessings

My daily planner could easily rank as the book second in importance to keeping me together, right after my Bible. I'm tech-savvy enough to plug my schedule into the cell-phone PDA I carry, but I've found that seeing my tasks and upcoming events laid out on paper gives me a better sense of how full my schedule may be during a given week.

I live by a to-do list, which, in essence, serves as a crutch to keep me from wandering aimlessly through my day. I've learned that with so much to keep up with between my, my husband's, and our two active kids' schedules, without something to guide me I'd be going in four different directions all at once. (Does this sound like your life on some days too?)

My list, which I craft each night and add to the next day's calendar, helps me feel productive and competent, and, I must admit, in control. Somewhere deep inside I fear that my inadvertently missing a volunteer reading day in my son's classroom would mar him for life, or forgetting a live radio interview with a major station could eternally blemish my career. Add to that mix the need to drive kids to and from church or school functions and extracurricular activities, and my own (limited) social calendar, and I'm sure you're nodding in full understanding.

Yet one fall afternoon about four years ago, my plans were altered by an incident around which I couldn't maneuver. A neighbor called me on my cell phone after I had picked my son and daughter up from school and suggested that I not rush home. There had been a car accident near our neighborhood, and the driver had hit a transformer that left most of the homes in the area without electricity.

The kids and I just happened to be on the way to children's choir rehearsal at church — a two-hour venture I had already plugged into my schedule. Afterward, instead of racing home to get the night-before-school routine underway as usual, I took my time, allowing the kids to eat out and running a few errands. But when the school-night bedtime hour approached and my husband called with the update that we still had ho power, I began to stress.

This meant my daughter would be late finishing her homework and I'd fall behind on checking emails I needed to review for a work-related project. My son would be late taking his bath, which meant he'd be late getting to bed and grumpy the next morning. I'd have to get up earlier in the morning to figure out what we'd all wear and (if the electricity was back on) iron it quickly so we'd still have time for breakfast. I sighed. This seemingly minor inconvenience would cost me precious time.

I drove home slowly and tried to tap into the excitement the kids were feeling about having hung out on a school night like summer break had returned. Yet, as I steered the car into our unusually dark neighborhood, my frustration returned. Before I had a chance to express my exasperation, though, my then seven-year-old daughter gasped and clasped her hands together. She was awestruck by the darkness that blanketed everything, save for the steady beam of our headlights.

"It's so quiet! I've never seen our neighborhood so still before!"

I pulled into our driveway and unbuckled my preschoolage son, while my daughter leapt from the backseat of the sedan and raised her eyes.

"Look at the sky! Look at the beautiful stars!"

She looked up at me, and thanks to the glow cast by the stars, I could see her wide smile.

"They were probably there all the time, but because of all the lights, I never noticed them before, Mommy. They're lighting up the sky!"

Her joy caught me by surprise, and led me to stargaze too. She was right; the stars *were* beautiful. I squeezed her hand and thanked her for making me notice them.

How silly I had been to waste time worrying about a minor inconvenience to my schedule. My daughter's excitement over natural elements I had taken for granted and failed to see reminded me that God often speaks to us through his little angels. I'm guessing I wasn't the only mom or professional grumbling that night about how long it was taking the power company to return things to normal. In my case, God used my daughter to show me that life happens, and even when circumstances are challenging or inconvenient, we can discover something beautiful or worthwhile. He spoke through the inky silence of his sky that night too, using those shimmering stars to signal that he had everything under control, even my still-full to-do list. Would I have noticed and "heard" him if I hadn't had a little help?

I unlocked the door that evening and ushered the kids inside, all the while praying that the person who had been involved in the car accident earlier that day was okay. Then I thanked God for allowing my daughter and me to see the gems in what I had considered an irritating interruption. What a comfort to remember that God controls all of your life, even when you are stuck in traffic, having your last nerve plucked waiting in a line, or wanting to scream at a customer service representative who puts you on "hold" for what seems like a trip to the moon and back. Remember that even in those situations God is speaking. Look for him and listen for him. He may be ready to share with you an answer you've been waiting for a while to hear, or maybe, as in my case, he simply wants to tell you to slow down and enjoy every step of the journey.

Learning to Listen

Memorize the verse below and recite it every time you find yourself sidetracked or impatient for answers:

Ecclesiastes 3:11: "He has made everything beautiful in its time."

Prayer

Dear God, wherever I find myself today, I give thanks that you're here with me. You know my frustrations, my fears, and the deepest desires of my heart. You know me better than I know myself. Rather than viewing any of the seasons or even days of my life as wasted, interrupted, or too full, I celebrate each moment that you grant. Help me to hear you speaking in these moments and reveal to me what you want me to do or what you would have me learn. Amen.

8

Competing Voices

When was the first time you remember a competitive spirit rearing its head in your life? For many of us, it may have been during a bout of sibling rivalry or when another child seemed to be stealing our attention or taking our place. Or maybe it was on the playground, during a game or sport at which you wanted to shine.

Undoubtedly, as you aged, the competitions grew more complex, and they stopped being primarily with other people. Often, we compete with ourselves, with much of the battle taking place inside our heads or with the still-small voice inside that we sometimes try to ignore.

The internal struggle can be the biggest of all, and it's the one that happens to be never-ending. We second-guess our decisions if it seems a friend, an acquaintance, or a family member has chosen better. We doubt whether we have what it takes to accomplish the dreams that fill our hearts. We wrestle with being good enough, smart enough, or faithful enough to someday hear our Lord smile at us and tenderly tell us, "Well done, my daughter."

The negative voices that pierce our hearts, crush our

spirits, or paralyze us with insecurity are fierce. They attack our sense of self-worth and cause us to forget that God's grace is more than enough. We may know from experience or simply from studying his Word that God always speaks life and offers blessings, but often our doubts and fears keep those truths from settling into our hearts.

Many of us fill the space that the Holy Spirit would otherwise use to give us a sense of knowing with the "stuff" of life — work, caring for family, social activities. Often these priorities leave us believing we'll never measure up. When Abraham's wife, Sarah, was unable to bear a child, she found herself in just this place.

God had seen Sarah and her husband through many trials and had granted them blessings that likely left others envious (Gen. 12 – 13). God had even given her a new name as a symbol of his love. She went from being called Sarai to Sarah, which means "princess."

Still, with all the women around her bearing children and receiving respect because of their multiple sons and daughters, Sarah couldn't drown out the inner voice that taunted her for being infertile. That voice told her, despite God's faithfulness, that she would always be inferior until she gave Abraham a son. Never mind that God had promised Abraham that he and Sarah would have a child. They were old now, and he must have changed his mind. At least that's what that competing voice insisted.

During biblical times, women who couldn't bear children were considered cursed or under punishment. Sarah knew she had done nothing wrong. Maybe, she told herself,

God meant for her servant, Hagar, to bear the child for Abraham. That would be close enough, wouldn't it? Sarah allowed that reasoning to muffle the promises of God she knew by heart and the memories of ways he had miraculously blessed her in the past.

Haven't we all done this? Despite the evidence from a recent blessing or victory, we get stuck in the here and now, impatient that God doesn't seem to be speaking to our need or answering when we call. What we aren't considering is that map that I mentioned in the introduction of this book. While we're restless for God to respond to our cries, he's surveying the landscape of our world and determining whether our requests fit with our destiny and with the long-term results he's trying to orchestrate in our relationships, our community, our churches, the nation, and the world. Just as we sometimes lose sight of God's global perspective, Sarah did too.

Her maid Hagar slept with Abraham at her insistence and gave birth to a son. But instead of giving Sarah the peace she longed for, the baby's birth caused her insecurities and shame to plague her more. She must have realized that she had taken matters into her own hands without God's consent.

Still, in his own time, when Sarah was ninety, God granted her long-held desire. He blessed her and Abraham with a son, whom they named Isaac. Despite allowing her own will to trump God's plans, God honored his promise. That victory didn't come without heartache and regret, though, because by giving in to the voices of reason and convenience, she had caused strife and turmoil within her own family.

Like Sarah, we too are often vulnerable to the inner doubts and fears that tell us we're not smart enough, pretty enough, healthy enough, young enough, or wealthy enough to receive the desires God quietly planted in our spirit long ago. We allow those internal arguments to talk us out of trying something different, taking a chance, or stepping out on faith.

The best way to win the competition is with God's truth. When you feel that negative self-talk surfacing, don't ignore it. Listen to where its trying to lead and fight back with God's Word. For every negative thought that fills your mind, speak a word of Scripture. When that voice tells you that you can't, declare in your heart or out loud that you can do all things through Christ who strengthens you (Phil. 4:13). When your thoughts drift to times in the past that you've failed and you begin to get that sinking feeling that you'll mess up again, remind yourself that Christ's death gave you victory over anything that seeks to kill God's purpose for your life. Because of his sacrifice, you are more than a conqueror (Rom. 8:37).

Learning to listen to God requires that you train yourself to use his Word as your shield. It makes you strong when you feel weak; it keeps you focused when you wander off track; it helps you attack negativity with God's positive power.

Certainly all of us have days when we're in the dumps and nothing seems to be going well. We're human. Rather than letting those times overwhelm you and get you stuck in a rut, decide to praise him. The simple act of giving God thanks will neutralize the voices that are seeking to drag you down, and in doing so, create space for you to receive God's direction and blessings.

Competing with yourself is always more challenging than competing with others. Winning this battle is huge. The more we trust the God who brought us this far along on our journey, the more we'll trust ourselves. When we trust the person God is shaping us into, we can trust that his voice won't lead us astray.

Fight the competing voices of doubt, fear, and sarcasm with the fierce Word of God, and in doing so, allow God to speak into your life.

Scripture

Psalm 59:16: But I will sing of your strength, in the morning I will sing of your love; for you are my fortress, my refuge in times of trouble.

Psalm 77:11 – 12: I will remember the deeds of the Lord; yes, I will remember your miracles of long ago. I will meditate on all your works and consider all your mighty deeds.

Prayer

Dear Lord, I am pulled back and forth so much that I am confused and sometimes paralyzed. Please speak to my heart and give me clear signs of the path that you want me to take. Help me to love myself unconditionally, so that the more I trust in you, I can trust who you've created me to be and do what you want me to do. Amen.

part 3

Be Real,
Be Still, and
Be In Tune

Be Real

It's human nature to gain confidence from our degrees, our street smarts, or our knowledge of the Bible, but these attributes don't lead God to treat us better than our sisters who didn't finish high school, have never left their native cities, or are brand new Christians still figuring out how to apply biblical truths to their daily lives. God is never impressed by the status we've gained through hard work or by chance; he's much more interested in our surrender. When we yield our will to his and get honest with ourselves about our faults, our fears, and our struggles, he listens. Authentic humility and honesty get his attention. They serve as the starting point for self-acceptance, which can lead to spiritual transformation and a real relationship with him.

Be Still

Sometimes when we most want to hear from God, we can't feel his presence. During these seasons, the wisest thing to do is ... nothing. Delving into his Word and trusting the promises we find there have to be enough to shore us up. If we park ourselves in the Scriptures and sing songs of praise while we wait for his response or action, God will honor that trust and obedience, and in the process, deepen our faith.

Be In Tune

Being determined to hear from God isn't as simple as increasing the volume on your radio or adjusting the receiver signal on your satellite. While God is always accessible, we can't force him to respond when and how we want. He is a God of wonder and surprises, and listening for his voice can be thrilling because we never know how he'll speak. Ultimately, getting and staying connected to him requires devotion and commitment. When we are in tune with God and realize that he's speaking, we will want to listen. We'll believe what God says and do as he tells us to do.

While I have defined these three qualities individually, you'll discover in this section how they work together when you begin to focus not only on serving God, but also on hearing him speak directly to your circumstances and to your eagerness to use them for a greater purpose. As we surrender to God and shed the facades that many of us maintain to give the impression that all is wonderful in our lives, we can begin to rest in God's promises — that he is a provider; he is a healer; he is more than enough to meet our needs. When we become still and embrace those promises, they will begin to shape who we are and draw us so deeply into relationship with the Creator that our lives begin to reflect his light and the words we speak begin to mirror the very ones he has spoken to our hearts.

9

What Matters Most

I love the biblical passage Jeremiah 1:5 in which God announces that he knew one of his servants before that prophet was formed in his mother's womb. It's a humbling reminder that the God we serve is not only all-powerful and all-knowing, but he's also personal. He cares for every member of his creation so much that he designed each of us by hand.

That's why it's important for me, and for you, to explore and become familiar with what's most important to him. He gives us fatherly wisdom in Proverbs about how to avoid foolish and evil things; clear steps in the New Testament books of Matthew, Mark, and Luke about how to devote our lives to him; and tools in Acts and Corinthians for helping us live in community and accord with our brothers and sisters in Christ and all of humanity.

God reveals through his living Word that what matters most to us should be the same things that matter most to him—his divine plan for drawing people to him and giving them eternal life, loving people everywhere, and fulfilling our God-given purpose.

It's no coincidence that love is the greatest command-
ment. It trumps all else in God's eyes. When we love with
our whole heart — sacrificially and vulnerably, and often
until it hurts — we are modeling the example set by Jesus,
whose life and death were built on this foundation. Let's be
real — this isn't as easy as it sounds. Sometimes we fail to
meet this standard because achieving it and maintaining
it leaves us feeling like doormats. We feel weak and used
rather than empowered and giving.

Add to the struggle of building solid, loving relationships the challenges you may have recently faced in trying
to pursue your purpose. Our nation's ailing economy, disappearing jobs, home foreclosures, and personal tragedies
have left people everywhere anxious. If you haven't faced
losses, you may be stressed in trying to dodge them.

During seasons of turmoil, we have to fight even harder
to stay focused on whose we are and on who we desire to
be. This is the perfect time to decide, if you haven't already,
to make your relationship with God the top priority in your
life. Decide to develop a friendship with him. When you put
him first, you can be confident that he will provide for all of
your needs, be present with you in all seasons (whether you
feel it or not), and work in your life with your best interest
at heart.

The bonds of love and trust between friends breed a
sense of security that can't be purchased or manufactured.
Taking your relationship with God to a deeper, more com-
mitted level will elevate your life on all fronts. Think about
your relationships with the friends or relatives you are

. closest to. You know because of who they are and how they feel about you, that they will do certain things for you simply because they love you. You can trust some of them with your dreams and others with your secrets. No matter what, they have your back. Now imagine that same relationship with Christ, and add in the fact that he's all-powerful and all-knowing. That means you can relax. He's got your back.

What matters most in all we do is finding out who Christ is calling us to be in the time we have been allotted to grace the planet. Hours can't be put on pause and the days of our lives can't be refunded. It's important to stop procrastinating and apply God's wisdom to every facet of your life.

As we learn about and experience God's love, we become more loving. The more love we share, the more we find ourselves fulfilled. This sense of satisfaction won't necessarily come in the form of the glitz the world adores, but will instead reveal itself through the pure intentions and unassuming wisdom that only God can provide.

Consider the life of Mary, the mother of Jesus. She was a young Jewish girl following the tradition of her day by preparing to marry her fiancé and start a family. By all accounts, Mary was a nice, obedient young woman who wasn't caught up in fads or in being part of the right crowd. She was focused on living a life pleasing to God.

Still, she had to have been awestruck when the angel of the Lord visited her and informed her that she had been chosen to be the mother of the Savior of the world. She asked what this would mean for her impending marriage, and when the angel reassured her that God was also speaking to Joseph, her fiancé, she accepted this honor without much fuss or glee.

She didn't run and tell her parents, seek out her best girlfriend for advice, or confide in Joseph. Instead, Mary let all she had been told settle in her soul. She must have prayed to God for the courage to handle the rumors and gossip that were sure to surface about how and when she had become pregnant. She must have prayed that God's promise to soften Joseph's heart toward her would be successful. Whatever doubts or fears she may have had, Mary didn't waver in her commitment to do as God asked. Somehow she knew that this great honor he had given her was worth any burden she might bear or status she might lose. She knew what mattered most and allowed that truth to lead her.

The one thing Mary did do, after learning from the angel Gabriel that her elderly cousin Elizabeth was also with child, was make a long trip across the plains to visit Elizabeth. Maybe she had been intending to share her wondrous news with this woman she considered a friend and mentor. Before she could utter a word, however, Elizabeth knew something special had happened to Mary, because when Mary entered Elizabeth's home, the baby in Elizabeth's womb leapt. That experience confirmed for Mary that in accepting this assignment from God, she was walking in her purpose.

A British track star reminded me of the importance of spiritual priorities several Olympics ago. Tasha Danvers-Smith was a serious contender for a gold medal in the 2004 Summer Olympic Games in Greece when she discovered she was pregnant. Colleagues and others urged her to abort the baby and go for the 400-meter gold since this was a once-in-a-lifetime opportunity to make history and establish a financially rewarding career, but Tasha bowed out.

In interviews with the media, Tasha later acknowledged that she and her husband, who was also her coach, had briefly considered this option. She was the family's primary breadwinner. If she didn't race and win, they would struggle, possibly for a long time. She had some serious consequences to consider.

Her day-to-day realities caused her to weigh her options. As easy as it may be to judge, that's human nature. If you're an actress, you want to win the Academy Award. If you sing, you envision a Grammy engraved with your name. If you work for a major corporation, you may hunger to be at the top of the list for a promotion and/or raise. If you're an educator, you might crave the honor of being selected "Teacher of the Year."

But like Jesus' mother Mary, and Tasha Danvers-Smith, it's always wisest to view our priorities in the context of God's will. Tasha gave up her spot on the Olympic team after wrestling with the decision and remembering Matthew 16:26 (NLT): "And what do you benefit if you gain the whole world but lose your own soul?" That verse became her answer. She gave birth to a healthy boy the following year, and in 2008, her son Jaden watched as she won a bronze medal for the 400 meter in the Beijing Olympics.

Over the course of our lives, we too may be tempted by opportunities to choose between an immediately rewarding path versus a less-glamorous road of commitment to our beliefs. When you're torn about which choice is right, or which of two seemingly great choices is the wisest, ask God to show you. If your probing and praying still doesn't yield a clear answer and you are confident that you are pursuing God's will rather than basing your decision on what feels right and good to you, you can trust that whatever route you choose, God will use it to yield blessings. The key in these instances is to make sure you have tuned out the voices and opinions of everyone around you so that God's Word and will can take center stage. It's critical to remember that what he believes and is calling you to do is what matters most. Loving him and serving him with your life should be your top priorities.

You can always trust that if you keep God as your guide, the route you feel led to pursue will be the safest and the surest. Despite the roadblocks or distractions you may encounter, keep talking to God. Ask him for guidance, clarity, courage, and a heart like his. By putting God first in your life, you can be certain that however your journey ends, he will applaud you for how you ran the race as well as for crossing the finish line.

Learning to Listen

For the next week, speak this affirmation aloud:

If God is love, and I am God's child, I am the living, breathing essence of love. May I be unselfish with the love I possess, sharing it wisely yet freely, and may I always keep God as my first priority in my daily life, especially when making decisions, or simply having fun.

10

Losing to Gain

My son surveyed his bedroom and shook his head. Sorry, he told me, but there was nothing he could part with that day. Yes, he wanted gifts for Christmas, and yes, he knew he needed some space to store what he would receive. But he couldn't bring himself to give away or throw away anything, not even the action figures and other toys with missing pieces.

At five or six years old, he couldn't articulate why, but he clearly had a vested interest in clinging to this stuff. It was *his*, and he had happy memories of playing with these things. How could I ask him to say good-bye?

Yet, saying good-bye is what life sometimes requires. We have to let go of one thing in order to gain another. My mother shared that wisdom with me in our last conversation, a few days before her unexpected death. Little did I know that her advice would be her parting gift before she graduated to heaven.

I had been wrestling with a tough decision, unable to decide what might be the best option. Mama urged me to consider the long-term gains of following the path my heart said to pursue, versus choosing the safer alternative about which I already had some reservations.

In the five years since her death, I've relied on the concept of losing to gain, combined with prayer, to help me navigate some life-altering terrain. I've given up a journalism career I loved to devote more time to writing books. I've removed myself from unhealthy friendships to invite more positive and creative energy into my world. I've put some dreams on hold in order to fully enjoy the dreams that are presently unfolding right in front of me.

My list could go on, but rather than reading mine, I'd like you to reflect for a few minutes on the meaningful sacrifices you've made. I'm sure you can recall times you've wrestled with the pros and cons of a decision or said no to one course of action in order to turn another avenue into a yes. Where are you in that process today? Are you like my son, holding onto things of which you are fond, when you could have room for something you'd truly love if you'd just let go?

Losing sounds scary; but when we consider this choice in the context of our faith, it should instead be exhilarating. The bad habits, addictions, pride, low self-esteem, superwoman complex, toxic relationships, or material possessions God is pushing us to release can't compete with all that awaits us when we're obedient. These inappropriate things have for far too long filled space inside of us that belongs to the divine. Yet, that truth is hard to trust until we learn to trust God more each and every day. In biblical times, whenever God moved his people or prophets from one place to another, he promised to go with them. Sometimes he hovered above, in the form of a cloud.

Just as I stood in my son's bedroom doorway, overseeing his struggle to make room for Christmas treasures, God is standing at attention, beckoning you to make more room for him and for his will in your heart. Sure, you'll be scared. I often am, even as I'm leaping into a new arena or opportunity. What helps me leap is the knowledge that God is my safety net. He guarantees you that same support.

My son eventually relented that day and after much thought and struggle found quite a few items he no longer wanted. He cleared his bookshelf of "baby books" he had long ago stopped reading and created a pile of titles we could donate to a youth literacy program. By the time he was done (this process didn't last longer than a few minutes), he was proud of himself. He had made room for a few new things. Isaiah 43:19 tells us that God wants to do a new thing in us too. But like my son, we have to risk releasing the comfortable and familiar to make way for it.

I prayed for months and months before I made the decision to leave my long-time newspaper job, which included penning a weekly spirituality column that I loved writing. Some of the people closest to me questioned whether I was sure I wanted to give up the recognition and respect this work brought me. What drove me to pursue a change was not the thought of losing what I had, but God's whispers that gave me a preview of what he might have in store. I knew I had to open my fist and release the good things I was clinging to so my life and career could take off in new directions and lead me to new experiences that could be just as rewarding, if not more. God began making me uncomfortable where I was — writing stories wasn't quite as fulfilling; the columns seemed to become repetitive; and I began to feel as if I could do my job on autopilot. For a daily news journalist, that wasn't good.

Eventually I realized the job wasn't the problem; it was me. I sat at my desk at the newspaper one morning and turned on my computer as usual. While I waited for it to warm up, this feeling — this "knowing" — came over me as clearly as if God had spoken. My time here was up, it said. If I kept sitting in this seat, at this desk, I was taking up space that now belonged to someone else, because God was ready to move me on to new adventures.

That experience rattled me; it shook my comfort zone. However, I didn't make rash moves. I still tested what I felt I was being led to do with prayer and with the counsel of wise friends who also prayed on my behalf. I tapped on other doors, testing which might open. About six months after that memorable inner dialogue, I finally made the leap.

The day I submitted my resignation, I had no doubts that it was the right time and the right thing to do. I had loosely mapped out a plan for establishing a freelance writing and consulting career that would give me more time with my young children and more time to write books, but I didn't have a two- or three-year roadmap for guaranteed success. I simply had the faith that if God had compelled me to take this leap, he would provide the wind I needed to soar.

I left my boss's office that morning with a peace that

surprised me. I knew then that I had heard God correctly, and I was thankful I had obeyed.

God never forces his way. If you'll let go of whatever is necessary to deepen your relationship with him, God will reveal more of himself and more of his purpose for your life. Try him and prepare for breathtaking surprises.

Learning to Listen

Starting today and for the next two days, spend time in the morning or evening reciting aloud the following verses:

Jeremiah 29:11 – 12 (NET): "For I know what I have planned for you," says the Lord. "I have plans to prosper you, not to harm you. I have plans to give you a future filled with hope. When you call out to me and come to me in prayer, I will hear your prayers."

After reading, sit quietly with no distractions. Close your eyes and breathe deeply and slowly. Do not utter words or speak to God silently. Your breath is your prayer.

At the end of the process, find paper and a pen and answer these questions:

What does God want me to give up so I can grow closer to him?

If I let go of the things that I know aren't good for me, what's the worst that can happen? What is the best?

Will I trust God enough to lead me where he wants to take me?

After you have honestly answered these questions, pray the prayer below and rejoice that God has heard.

Prayer

Dear God, you are the knower of all things. Help me to trust that whatever I release into your hands is safe. Help me to relax in your care and watch you work. Give me courage to lose in order to gain. I want more of you, Father. I want to hear your voice and allow you to consistently speak to my heart. Thank you for being all I really need—today, tomorrow, and forever. Amen.

11

Eyes on the Prize

The day I received a copy of my first novel in the mail, I cradled it. Twenty-five years after declaring in third grade that I someday would write a book, I was holding the prize in my hands.

It seemed surreal. This dream I had been talking about achieving off and on for years had finally become a reality. With two young children under the age of four, a full-time job, and a husband who was working and attending grad school on the weekends, the writing of this book had almost seemed impossible to accomplish. I had completed two drafts before my son was born, but knew from talking with a friendly publishing professional that the novel needed more work. I put it aside to care for my son after his birth during the summer of 2001 and didn't think much about it in the busyness that consumed my life.

When my little man was about nine months old and had settled into a comfortable routine, my interest in revising my manuscript returned. I hadn't looked at it in months, but I knew when I picked it up I'd be starting from the beginning. The thought of trying to carve out time in front of the computer while juggling everything else left me weary.

Then one morning, at about 3:00 a.m., an uncomfortable thought startled me awake. I remember glancing at the clock ... during those days, sleep was golden. My son didn't usually wake until 6:00 a.m. — why was I wasting these precious few hours?

Here I was, on this quiet, dark morning, suddenly alert. My thoughts immediately turned to the notebook on my nightstand and the words I should be scribbling to revise my manuscript. Instead of getting up, though, I sank deeper into my pillow and willed sleep to come. In its place was a dreamlike vision of me in my eighties, sitting in a rocking chair with my great grandchildren at my feet, looking to me for inspiration. As each of them told me what they wanted to do with their lives, I encouraged them and urged them to make it happen.

I mentally shuddered. Something — which I consider the Holy Spirit — told me that if I kept procrastinating, I'd be giving those children hollow advice, with nothing more than sweet-sounding words to back it up. That voice told me that I couldn't authentically encourage those grandchildren — or before then, my own children — to pursue their dreams if I hadn't at least tried to achieve mine.

And then I began a dialogue with the Lord.

But how? I don't have time.

Make time.

But when? I work long hours. I have two young children, a super-busy husband, and no family in the area.

How about now?

Now? As in 3:00 a.m.?

If not now, when?

And so I decided that rather than keep fretting or making excuses or trying to write at the end of a hectic day when my brain was fried and I no longer wanted to sit before a computer, I would rewrite my novel first thing in the morning, while the house was quiet and my thoughts were fresh.

God took me seriously. From that day forward, I woke up at 4:00 a.m. at least three times a week and wrote for two hours before going to work at the newspaper. Initially I'd set the alarm clock and place it across the room so I'd be forced to get up and turn it off before it disturbed my husband. Within weeks, however, I didn't need the clock to wake me. I was so excited about my progress and about each chapter that I was poring over and praying over that I found myself waking on my own.

It took me six weeks to finish rewriting my novel for the third time, and then it sat on a closet shelf for months because the publishing professional I had been working with didn't think it was quite ready. I knew I had a lot of room for improvement as a writer, but I didn't have the time or resources just then to invest in honing my craft. I put the book out of my mind and resumed my routine activities. At the very least, I told myself, I could tell my children and grandchildren I had finished what I started.

But God operates in his own timing and through his own methods. He used a newspaper column I had written about a local woman's journey of faith to interest an editor in my work. Brian called in early 2003 and asked to read whatever I had written, but I hesitated to send him *Speak to My Heart*—the title for my first novel. He kept asking, so at his insistence I did. When he informed me a month or so later that the publishing house he represented was interested in buying the manuscript, I rejoiced.

These days, as I race to meet official publishing deadlines and work with booksellers to schedule signings, I gratefully recall those "firsts," because my path was so clearly mapped out by God. He planted the seeds, I (haphazardly) watered them, he remained faithful, and when I disciplined myself, he allowed my dream to flourish.

The thing you prize most or long for most may be nothing like mine. Selling books and eventually seeing them made into movies may not be on your wish list, but whatever your desire, the key is to ask God to bless and guide you to fulfillment. Don't rate your success on measures offered by the world. Had I never taken my book off the closet shelf, I would have at least been able to have that conversation with my great grandchildren that I saw in my half-awake state that morning in 2002. God blessed me by granting me the gift of seeing that first novel published and for having it serve as the launch pad for a career I had dreamed of.

Much of the media (not the publications I've worked for) seeks to convince us that the prizes most worth pursuing in this life are based on physical beauty or bank account balances. Or maybe in your particular circle it's having the most prestigious degree or the cutest or smartest kids. The prize fighting could be taking place in your church, with members competing to sing the most solos, assist the senior pastor, or direct the Sunday school program. Wherever a brass ring is dangled before you, beware of its potential danger. Test it against the deepest desires and longings of your heart, the ones that embedded themselves there before the noise of life, or the opinions of your friends, family, colleagues, and the world caused you to stuff them deep inside.

Your prize is whatever God is calling you to develop, create, or share. It is the activity or the thing that brings you deep satisfaction in an unselfish way. We're not all called to exhibit our prize on the world's stage. Wherever he places us, we must do as he asks. In the process, we'll realize that the greatest prize of all is an anointed touch from him.

When we stay grounded in that knowledge, seeking first to serve God and become his friend, we can trust him with our needs and our wishes. Only you can decide what kind of relationship you want with God. Any winner—whether of a sporting title, Grammy or Stellar Award, Pulitzer Prize, or church honor—can share with you the sacrifices, discipline, and focus that were required to garner first-rate recognition and praise.

God is asking no less from those of us who want to intimately communicate with him. Tell God what you'd like to accomplish. Be honest with him about the challenges and fears you face as you ponder how to move forward. Ask for his help, but don't stop there. Keep seeking and searching for ways to achieve your goals. God will bless your effort by sprinkling everyday miracles along your journey that you may consider routine or good luck.

Rest in the fact that because he knows your heart's

desire, it will come into being. When his knowing merges with our yearning, victory is assured. There is no greater prize.

Learning to Listen

Write a letter to yourself in which you declare where you want to be a year from now in regard to your relationship with God and the steps you'll take to achieve this goal, such as more frequent prayer, more Bible study time, or studying a particular aspect of God's nature. Include how you'll apply what you're learning about God and about your particular pursuit, such as making more efforts to love and appreciate others or making a date with yourself every Saturday morning to spend two hours on working toward some aspect of your goal. Share your list with a friend or close relative who won't betray your confidence. Ask that person to hold you accountable. Put today's date on next year's calendar and plan a special dinner six months or a year from now to review your progress and to celebrate how far you've come.

12

Standing Alone

Popularity contests should end in high school, but they don't. Employees jockey to be liked by their bosses; adult children seek to be favored by their parents; and even in church we see folks clamoring for attention from their ministers and fellow members. No one engaged in this behavior would likely say they're seeking attention or affection. They also may not realize that what they're truly after is acceptance, or validation that they are special.

Indeed, that's often what's driving the stars of the reality shows we see filling the schedule on just about every station on TV, from cable channels to the major networks. Many people want their fifteen minutes of fame — from *The Bachelorette* series in which a single woman dates numerous men to find the proverbial "Mr. Right" to the *Real Housewives* series, which features married and single (supposedly) wealthy women living glamorous lives in their respective cities. And once they achieve some notoriety, they do indeed increase in importance in the world's eyes. Fame somehow makes them better. By God's measure, however, what's more important than standing out is knowing what you stand for — and often standing for truths that may require you to stand alone.

A woman I know well is one of three siblings who grew up in a household with parents who took them to church and modeled what it means to serve God and honor him with your life. Their family life wasn't perfect (as is the case for most of us), but her parents gave them every opportunity to know God and develop their own relationship with him.

It has been surprising over the years to see how only one of the siblings—my acquaintance—has allowed that training to influence how she lives. She loves God, and she and her husband are raising their children to love him too. She doesn't carry her Bible everywhere she goes or spout Scriptures with every hello. Yet her siblings think she's strange. They call her "holier than thou" and ridicule her for her beliefs and how she practices her faith. Sometimes they hurt her feelings with their comments and sting her heart with their actions. Even so, she treats them with respect.

She has decided to "love them to life" rather than give in to the temptation to change who she is to make them feel more comfortable around her, or give in to the anger that sometimes consumes her when she is being mistreated. It saddens her that they aren't emotionally closer, but from my detached perspective, I see how that can happen.

Darkness and light can't coexist. That's not to say that her siblings have denied there is a God and refused to serve him; this doesn't seem to be the case. After all, everyone has a different relationship with the Creator and differing levels of faith. Instead, in the siblings' case, it seems God has become irrelevant to their lives, or maybe just an afterthought. When they are around her and it's obvious that for her God is front and center, it's hard for them to let their guards down. What they seem to miss is that their sister isn't trying to judge or condemn them. She simply wants to be in a relationship with them and love them as they are. They can't seem to offer her that same unconditional acceptance at this point.

For this woman, the decision has been easy. Choosing God has meant that she's had to find joy and contentment from relationships formed outside of her family. Friends from church, work, and her community have become like relatives. She asks God to see her through the occasional loneliness she confronts as she grieves that status of her strained bond with her siblings. Then she turns it over to him, puts on an authentic smile, and trusts God to help her always do what is right and good in his eyes.

Standing alone in our faith is to be expected on occasion. We won't always make everyone happy with our decisions or agree with the status quo, even in environments where there have been no issues in the past. Sometimes God calls us to stop strolling through life or going through the motions in church or in our relationship with him so that we can be alert for what he wants to do through us next.

You may be familiar with the journey of Moses, whose mother, Jochebed, must have been paying attention to God. During the era in which Moses was born, a new king had begun his reign and had grown uncomfortable with the increasing number of Hebrews. Though the Hebrews were slaves under Egyptian control, the king feared their numbers would grow so great that they would attempt to overthrow him and his fellow Egyptians.

He first ordered two Hebrew midwives to kill all Hebrew boys as soon as they were born. But the women feared God. They avoided following the command by telling the king that the Hebrew women had easy births, and by the time they arrived, the babies were already delivered. This example, in Exodus 1, highlights women who were brave enough to stand alone. They could have been jailed or killed for their disobedience. Instead, God blessed each of them with families of their own.

Then the king demanded that every male child born to the Hebrews be thrown into the Nile River. Imagine the fear and anguish every pregnant Hebrew woman must have faced upon learning about this new law.

Jochebed cradled the boy she had given birth to and somehow knew she couldn't obey this command. She hid her son and nursed him for as long as she could. I imagine that this wasn't a popular decision with Jochebed's husband, who would have feared for his life for disobeying the king. He may have complained or murmured about her stubbornness. If he did, then Jochebed would have had to stand against him to keep the baby alive. Somehow she knew this infant boy needed to survive.

When he was three months old and harder to keep quiet, Jochebed made him a sturdy basket and tucked him inside before sending it down the Nile. She wasn't sure what would happen to him, but anything had to be better than his certain fate if she handed him over. Plus, she had faith that the God she loved and obeyed also loved her son and would protect him wherever he floated on the river.

God honored Jochebed's trust in him by allowing the basket to coast along a particular route, where the king's daughter discovered it and fell in love with the baby inside. She named him Moses.

Moses' biological sister, Miriam, had run along the riverbanks to see what would become of her baby brother. When she saw that he had been gleefully discovered by Pharaoh's daughter, Miriam approached the woman and offered to help find a Hebrew woman to nurse the baby. Who knows whether the king's daughter suspected that Jochebed was Moses' mother? The fact that she honored Jochebed with the privilege of being her own son's paid nurse, thereby reconnecting them, is a testament to God's faithfulness. (Read the story firsthand in Exodus 2:1–10).

Whatever you may be facing, even a circumstance where you know God is asking you to display courage and abiding love in the face of rejection, do as he says. Know that even when it looks like things won't get better or that your worst nightmare has come true, you can cling to God's promises because over and over again we see the ways in which he delivers his children. Consider the words of the gospel song by Maurette Brown Clark that declare "it ain't over until God says it's done."

Standing alone isn't easy. It can lead to loneliness, ridicule, embarrassment, and sometimes brokenhearted-ness. When we stand for what is right, however, we can be confident that God's strength will help us endure. He blesses those who are obedient to his principles, from men like Noah who withstood being laughed at to build an ark during a drought, to women like Lydia, who heard the Word of God and decided to have her entire family live for Christ. Jochebed's decision to stand alone in disregarding the king's law allowed her to save the life of the child who would one day lead the Hebrews from slavery.

Talk of the faith and courage described in this chapter can cause women who are on the fence about yielding to God to cringe about jumping in feet first. They fear what they'll lose by trying to follow Christ. They worry about how their lives will have to change. Life certainly won't be perfect and easy and fun-filled simply because you've decided to live for Christ. But isn't that the case anyway? The beauty of opening your heart to him, and of accepting the changes this decision brings, is that the gains that come with loving him and serving him more than compensate for the hollow existence you'll see disappear.

Learning to Listen

Ask God to show you what it means to stand alone and when you need to do it. Don't take stances just because. Act only as God leads you to and otherwise allow him to quietly use you to draw others to him, not so much through your words as through your actions.

Scriptures

1 Corinthians 15:1 – 2: Now, brothers, I want to remind you of the gospel I preached to you, which you received and on which you have taken your stand. By this gospel you are saved, if you hold firmly to the word

I preached to you. Otherwise, you have believed in vain.

2 Timothy 2:15: Do your best to present yourself to God as one approved, a workman who does not need to be ashamed and who correctly handles the word of truth.

13

Grace for a Sister's Journey

When the pearl earrings arrived, I cried.

A long-time friend had been window-shopping in New York, and when she saw the multicolored, teardrop jewelry, she decided I should have it. Three days later, I opened the gift-wrapped box and read a note, which explained that I had blessed her with a message of hope and friendship in one of my books and she wanted to return the favor.

And blessed I was, because the pearls arrived on the day I needed them. I was in the midst of a private pity party, questioning the value of my various pursuits, including efforts to sync my long-time journalism career with my new role as an author. I had been wrestling again and again in my head and in my soul as to whether anything I penned as an author really made a difference.

If I hadn't given in to the blues on that day, God could have brought back to my remembrance all of the times, again and again, that he had shown me that my writing mattered. But on this day, Sharon's gift and note provided a timely reminder. Years later, whenever I glimpse the earrings or wear them to a special event, I'm reminded that she loves me, just because. How reassuring it is to know that the way she feels about me can't begin to compare to the emotion I evoke in God. He loves me too, just because.

When I pay attention, I readily find evidence of his adoration and protection. His grace makes me want to offer grace to others who need to be touched by an unexpected gift of love — overtly or subtly — through prayer, spiritual guidance, or offers to befriend and support them with no strings attached. I've experienced this on many occasions in my own life and have witnessed it with friends and family.

One of my friends was surprised recently after she extended what she considered a minor act of kindness to a stranger and found *herself* the recipient of a blessing. Arnecia was heading toward her car when she saw a woman struggling with an overloaded cart of groceries. Others who passed by the woman ignored her obvious challenge in maneuvering through the parking lot with the basket, which was filled to the brim. The woman had to repeatedly stop to pick up and reposition items that fell from their bags. Arnecia approached her and asked if she needed help. The young woman was grateful for the offer and even more touched when Arnecia helped her unload the bags into her car. When the cart was empty, she reached into her purse and pulled out a restaurant gift card for my friend, a single mother. Despite Arnecia's protests, the woman insisted that Arnecia take it. The fifty dollar balance would more than cover dinner for my friend and her daughter at the moderately upscale restaurant it had come from. Arnecia hadn't wanted to do anything but extend a simple act of kindness. In return, she received her own measure of grace.

Incidents like this are whispers from God. They come to remind us, as often overwhelmed women — also known as wives, mothers, daughters, sisters, aunts, friends, or professionals — to stop making life complicated by trying to love "just right," when God is offering his *grace* to make everything right. He gives us enough of his unearned love to get us going, then gives us the free will to flourish. The problem is, many of us don't know, or don't remember, that it's there. We look in the mirror and see our flaws — too much weight, too little hair, too many wrinkles, too few credentials, too little money — when instead we should be peering into our souls. For that's where God's eyes go — into the deepest part of our being and into our hearts.

Even when he spots a bit of ugliness, envy, or deceit, he still loves us. He extends his grace and reminds us that as long as we're willing to try to be better, he's willing to help us.

We're not plastic dolls that can be processed through a recycling plant and spit out again as "brand new." This God who knew us before our mothers or fathers learned our gender or gave us names, created us to thrive as is, so that in our victories and failures we would yearn to keep our hearts attuned to his. He gave each of us a purpose and placed us in the physical bodies, earthly families, and particular circumstances that would best mold us into who he needs us to become.

It's important to know that we have a father like no other, who never tires of us, nor checks caller ID to avoid us when we want to talk, nor is he too busy to listen if we call on him at an hour when we can't wake anyone else. God is wise and gracious enough to help us navigate our confusion, anger, grief, or doubts, and he can articulate what we're feeling better than we can.

What is our task? To believe that because he loves us, that is enough! To get real and be real. To start looking where God looks (at your spirit) instead of where society tells you to look. It can be hard to accept the kind of grace-filled affection God offers from someone we can't see or touch. His presence is tangible, though, in the form of the call that comes when we're most in need of encouragement, the card received from a caring friend, the trusted advice or listening ear offered during the process of making a difficult decision, or the correction someone gives us when we get off track. As a familiar church saying goes, "He may not come when you want him, but he's always on time." Because God is on time, his showers of grace are always punctual too.

God is here. Always. The part of his heart that belongs to you is yours forever. He confirms this in Isaiah 49:16: "See, I have engraved you on the palms of my hands; your walls are ever before me."

When we grasp that truth and let it marinate in our spirits, it becomes easier to hear God even though God is not speaking in the loud, clear voice we all wish he'd use. He'll tap on the door to our hearts with a soothing word, a great idea, or a memory that makes us smile, and eventually, we'll recognize him walking through life with us.

The first step to making that kind of experience your routine reality is to accept that despite feeling unworthy of his grace, you can trust that God wants to communicate with you. You deserve this privilege, not because you've earned the right through years of serving in church or because you recently decided to follow him. He reminds us in Ephesians that we could never work hard enough to merit his favor (Eph. 2: 8 – 9). You are worthy simply because you're part of him. Accept his grace (or *more* of his grace) today and open your heart to the exciting opportunities that being his child can yield.

Learning to Listen

For the next seven days, replace every negative thought or thread of doubt that surfaces with this truth: *I am loved, no matter what I've done or failed to do. God's grace is sufficient for me.*

Make this your mantra. Tape it to a mirror, write it in your calendar, or post it wherever you'll see it most for at least a week. Don't just read the words you've written; say them out loud, and with firmness: "I am *loved*, no matter what I've done *or* failed to do. God's grace *is* sufficient for *me*." Your verbal declaration gives these words power. You are speaking aloud to yourself what God already has offered to your spirit. Today, begin opening yourself to receive this truth. By week's end, you'll be closer to believing that because of God's grace, you are loved unconditionally.

14

Take Time for You

I'm going away."

When a particular mentor-friend of mine utters those words, I know she's heading for a weekend of seclusion, where she can relax, read, and pray. Her favorite destinations are the mountains or the beach, but in a pinch she'll reserve a room at a local nondenominational retreat center, which in many ways resembles the bare-essentials cabin I slept in during my long-ago stay at a New Mexico monastery.

My friend gives herself permission to "steal away" whenever she finds herself getting anxious or stressed because she has been going nonstop or caring for others to the point of feeling drained. When she's overly busy, she knows she needs to be careful. She can't hear from God or operate in his will if she's burned out by the noise of life's trials, demands, and inconveniences. So she schedules her trip, shoots an email to her closest friends and family to let them know how long she'll be out of reach, and eagerly gets away to tune out the world.

Sometimes, she says, she just walks and enjoys the beauty of God's creation. That act alone gives her a visual reminder of God's care and attentiveness for all that he loves, including her. Often she'll take along a journal, in which she scribbles her thoughts about a current circumstance, notes concerns or questions, or pens prayers. Mostly, though, since she's alone and not forced to talk to anyone, answer her phone, or check email, she enjoys the silence that comes with just being. Her mind and body have a chance to get still, and so does her soul.

All this friend is doing is replicating the example she finds throughout the Scriptures. Jesus often made it a priority to spend time alone. Luke 6:12–13 details how he spent time with God before deciding which of his disciples would travel with him. The larger his following grew, the more important it became for him to steal away. According to the Scriptures, sometimes he talked to God, but just as often, he listened and rested in the Creator's presence.

For those of you who feel guilty at the thought of leaving your family, or of spending money on yourself for a hotel or retreat stay, feel the guilt now and let it go! If Jesus recognized and valued the importance of taking the time to restore himself with quiet, why shouldn't you? Envision a day or two away that allows you to focus on you and on your relationship with God. Consider how reconnecting with yourself and with your joy could help you return home eager to serve your family. Wouldn't that outcome be enough to justify your getaway?

When Jesus visited the home of the sisters Mary and Martha, and Martha complained about doing all of the work while Mary sat at his feet, Jesus praised·Mary for knowing how to care for her needs. Clearly, she wanted to be close to the Savior; she wanted to sit at his feet and soak in all of the wisdom she could. Who knows how Mary later applied what she learned from Jesus that day? Martha had the same access, yet having used her time differently, would she remember Jesus' conversation as clearly and know what was expected of her as one of his disciples?

Martha was living out the principles of another Scripture that serves as a wonderful guide to what it takes to be a godly woman, but can also give us women heartburn: Proverbs 31:13–31. Read this passage and before you're halfway through, you may feel as if you'll never measure up. How could one woman do so much and do it so well? I've heard many women debate this issue, with resignation over the possibility that we females aren't made of the stuff today they were made of back then, or with the belief that surely this woman was wealthy enough to have help with managing everything.

Regardless, it's time we give ourselves a break. It's time that as we honor the service we're called to give to our families, we also honor ourselves as God's chosen vessels. God says in Jeremiah 29:13 that if we seek him with our whole heart, we will find him. He says in 1 Peter 5:7 to cast your cares on him.

None of this is possible if we don't believe we're worth it. When we give ourselves the freedom to treat ourselves well, that freedom will empower us with more love to give away. Believe it. Embrace it. Make time today to get away for some quiet time and do nothing but relax and rejuvenate.

While doing so, you'll find yourself delighting in the Lord and remembering what makes your heart sing.

Learning to Listen

Going away for a mini "retreat" by yourself for the first time can be intimidating, especially if you have young children at home or live in an area where you have little support for your family. But if you can, find at least one day on your calendar when you can take off work, decline to volunteer, find a sitter for the kids or leave the family and get away to a hotel, spa, or some other private space. One day alone is a start; two nights is better and three is ideal. By the third day, you'll be longing to return to your loved ones, but you also will have had enough time to clear your mind of everything that lingers on your to-do list, to give up fretting about the tasks you forgot to handle before taking time away, and to remember some of the things you enjoy about being you. Use this time to pray and ask God to rejuvenate every area of your life, from your health to your relationships to your finances to your self-image. Ask him to help you love him more and then reflect that love to everyone with whom you cross paths. Regularly schedule a mini-retreat—once a quarter, every six months, or whatever suits your needs and comfort level. Feel good about taking care of you. Your body is your temple and your mind is your greatest resource when it comes to connecting with God.

15

Feeling Invisible

At some point in your life, whether once or a hundred times, you've likely felt dismissed or nonexistent. Others may have unintentionally ignored you or purposely excluded you.

However the slight occurred, feeling invisible — in a professional setting, at a social event, or in a relationship — may have punctured your soul, or at the very least, left you wanting to *really* disappear. Feeling like you don't matter opens you up for doubts about your worthiness — whether you're smart enough, pretty enough, thin enough, educated enough, or simply good enough to deserve acknowledgement.

But God declares in Jeremiah 23:23 – 24 that he is always near, and none of us is invisible to him. He reminds us that when we feel the most disregarded and isolated, we should be encouraged, because he values those that are considered the "least of these" by others. In Matthew 10:30 he says he knows every hair on our head, and Psalm 56:8 reminds us that he's collecting every tear we shed.

If we believe the truth of these promises, then the times during which we question our significance — or allow someone else to do so—should be exactly what they are: minor slights we must sometimes endure. This is easier said than done, because the childhood cliché is incorrect: words can and do hurt, as can the absence of words when you need to hear them most. But learning how to turn to God when we're confronted with this issue is critical to learning to listen better and to hearing him speak.

When you feel like you've been overlooked, disregarded, not taken seriously, or misunderstood, talk to God about it. Study Scriptures that remind you that you are God's choice pearl and that your every thought and action matter to him. Among the many reminders throughout the Bible is Hebrews 13:5–6, in which God promises to always help us and never leave us.

As you train yourself to focus on God and what he says about you, he'll help you be less concerned about the attitudes, words, and actions of those who dismiss you.

One of my children's favorite movies a few years ago was the computer-animated hit *The Incredibles*. It features a family of superheroes—dad, mom, an infant son, a preteen son, and a teenage daughter—who, along with other superheroes, have been placed in a witness protection program of sorts and ordered by the government to live normal lives. Each member of this family has a specific superpower. The mom, for example, is known as Elastigirl and has the ability to stretch herself thin and fit into the tiniest of spaces. Dad is known as Mr. Incredible and has superhuman strength. Dash is the older son and can move at lightning speed. The daughter, Violet, has the ability to make herself invisible.

The children have been warned to never display their powers when they are away from home, and that suits the teenage Violet just fine, because she has no interest in "disappearing." She's just getting a sense of herself and wants to fit in with her peers. Being invisible is the last thing she wants to be known for. Like Violet, many of us don't realize — or we forget — what the Scriptures constantly remind us: we can never be hidden from or separated from God. Our Creator may shield us for a season for his own purposes or for our own sake. Sometimes what seems like invisibility is God's season of silent preparation.

Several passages in the New Testament, including Luke 8:41 – 48, detail how a woman described as having "an issue of blood" slips through the crowd of people pressing to get close to Jesus. She is not seen or heard, which is a good thing, because otherwise she would be sent back into exile. A woman with her condition was bound by the rules of her society to stay away from others.

If people in the crowd had known that this lady would be rubbing their shoulders and squeezing between them to touch the hem of Jesus' garment, they surely would have stopped her. She was invisible to the crowd that day, but even with a mass of noisy followers surrounding him, Jesus felt her touch.

In *The Incredibles*, when the family is attacked by an enemy, Elastigirl insists that her daughter Violet give up her desire to be seen and heard by all. She tells Violet to make herself disappear. A fearful Violet refuses. Yet when she obeys, she realizes that her strength lies in having the choice to be seen or not. She grasps that giving in to the need to sometimes be "less than" will help her survive.

Our strength often lies in our behind-the-scenes living, loving, and service too. Colossians 3:23 – 24 urges Christians to be sure that in our work we focus on honoring God rather than on trying to win the praise and favor of other people. The Gospel of Matthew also sets seeking favor from people in opposition to seeking favor from God: when we work hard to obtain the praise of men and women for our efforts, we already have received our reward; but when we give and serve in secret we will receive God's reward instead (Matt. 6:1 – 4).

When we hide God's words in our hearts and go about the business of loving others, obeying his will, and pursuing our purpose, we can trust God to elevate us and give us a new level of visibility when he believes it will serve us best. You are never invisible to God and neither are the longings of your heart. Sometimes a delay is for his purpose, and maybe it's a purpose that's much bigger than you. He may be using your experience to encourage someone else or preparing your response to your circumstances to change a life. Sometimes when it seems as if you're going unnoticed, it's simply that your gift speaks for itself until the need arises for your hard work and devotion to be spotlighted.

That was the case with Dorcas, a Christian woman also known as Tabitha, who is described in Acts 9 as beloved by all of her neighbors and relatives in Joppa. Dorcas wasn't a leader of her day, a queen, or prominent in any other way that would have drawn attention to her.

When Dorcas died, however, everyone who knew her

was devastated. The residents of Joppa heard that the apostle Peter was nearby and sent two men to beg him to come and pray over her. Peter didn't know Dorcas, but her friends and family elevated her from invisible to hero status by describing for the disciple how Dorcas had nurtured and cared for others. Widow after widow, young and old, arrived with the robes and other clothing Dorcas had made for them and their children when they were in need. It was obvious that this was a woman who had loved others selflessly, regardless of whether she was personally thanked or publically appreciated.

She may have been invisible to man, yet despite her lack of fame and reputation, Peter was moved by her strong and silent faith. He visited the bedroom in which her relatives and friends had lain her body and, to their joy and delight, brought her back to life.

Know that wherever you are and in whatever you're being faithful, God is with you, giving you life. When you're feeling invisible or taken for granted, he has his eyes on you and his hand in yours. Keep sharing your fears and concerns with him, and he'll send you reminders that even when you're not on stage, you're one of his superstars.

Scripture

*Jeremiah 23:23 – 24: "Am I only a God nearby,"
declares the Lord, "and not a God far away? Can anyone hide in secret places so that I cannot see him?"
declares the Lord. "Do not I fill heaven and earth?"
declares the Lord.*

Prayer

Dear Lord, sometimes I feel as if I don't measure up. I don't fit in and don't know what to do. I feel out of place, taken for granted, undervalued, and often ignored. Help me know that when I feel most invisible, you are near, working out circumstances for my good and for the benefit of others too. Amen.

16

Don't Despair

These are uncertain times.

That may sound like the opening line to one of the classic novels you may have read in high school or the beginning of a speech uttered by the current US president. These days, there's no such thing as job security, safe retirement funds, or corporate loyalty, and people aren't handling the changes well.

As I was writing this book, it seemed as if every week, and sometimes every couple of days, news reports filled the airwaves and other media with details about an entire family being wiped out by one of its members. People across the nation who have found themselves overstressed, taxed to the limit, or simply hopeless have made the most desperate of choices and not only ended their own lives, but also the lives of their children and spouses.

Yesterday a news broadcaster shared details about the death of a family in the Midwest. They had been found stabbed in their home in an apparent murder suicide. Today, I read a story online about a family of five in Maryland—a couple and their three children—who apparently died in the same fashion.

These incidents lead me to stop whatever I'm doing, wherever I am, and utter a brief prayer. Sometimes I pray for the victims' souls, sometimes I pray for mercy, and sometimes I just pray, "Lord, be with us." Sometimes, I simply ask why.

In times when we don't know what to make of a situation or where to turn, when we want to demand answers, but fear the truth might be too painful or too senseless, all we can do is look to Christ. As an old gospel hymn says, for some situations "we will understand it better by and by." In some instances, the "by and by" may be when we see our Lord and Savior face to face.

I've learned during moments of frustration, at times when I've taken two steps back for every single step forward, or when I've searched for a reason in the midst of senseless deeds, rejection, or heartache, that sometimes the only answer is Jesus. Sometimes the only source of strength is knowing that God sent his only beloved son to this planet for me—for all of us—so that we might have everlasting life.

Those words sometimes seem to fall on hardened soil, the winter kind that can't be penetrated without first being loosened. They sound good, but can they really heal our hearts and souls?

If you have declared that Jesus is your source of life, then yes. If you've decided to lose some things to gain others, then yes. If you've found the courage to not only call yourself his child, but also to accept the crosses that come with wearing the crown (or in our case the tiara), then you can find a way to smile through the tears. And when not quite smiling, you can go on without giving in to despondency and constant depression.

Because we're human we're going to fear, doubt, feel sad, and the like. But if Jesus lives, our sun still shines. If Jesus lives, we can trust that he'll see us through whatever we must face. This doesn't mean that you don't need help from other people. Sometimes counseling, or obtaining assistance from a physician or a caring friend who agrees to walk through your storm with you, is necessary.

Yet when we can't hear him, we have to remember that his silence is only temporary. When we feel like we've messed up too badly to be redeemed or forgiven, we have to remind ourselves that the Son still shines. When it seems like all we cared about and cherished is no more, we have to remember this. When the world crashes not once, but again and again, and again for others or for us, we have to remember that the Son still shines.

Jesus is our ray of light, our hope for tomorrow, the one who can transform all those experiences that have threatened to disfigure our beauty. We are still beautiful; God may just be transforming us to allow our beauty to resonate from a deeper place within than we imagined possible.

When we're in situations or around people who want to dim our light or squelch our joy, we have to be careful to remember its source. The light God supplies isn't as fickle as a flickering candle. It is steady and strong and serene. It is Jesus.

Hold on to that truth and remember that because he is the great "I Am," because he is the shining in our souls, despite what causes us temporary despair, he is prepared to speak a blessing over our lives that can eventually turn our soul-deep pain and our weeping into joy. Maybe not the jump-up-and-down cheerleader kind of joy, but the kind that comes with the peace of knowing that our help comes from the Lord and that as long as he is protecting and comforting us, we can rejoice that all we need will be supplied by him, including contentment, peace, support, friendship, and love (Ps. 121).

I think about this every time I recall a woman I met — a pastor's wife — who lost her entire family in a fiery car accident one Saturday morning. The only reason she wasn't with her husband and three young sons that day was because she had briefly gone in to work. When she arrived at the church the family attended to meet them as planned, she learned that the traffic accident she had passed nearby involved her husband's car. All had perished.

She wanted to die too. Somehow, though, she found the strength to visit the boys' school and comfort their fellow students with the assurance that these boys knew Christ and would dwell with him. God helped her to keep putting one foot in front of the other. She coped by trusting that if he had allowed her to live, there must be a purpose for it. She enrolled in divinity school. She took care of her emotional needs. She gave thanks that she had been blessed with such a beautiful family.

Even as God has walked through this tremendous loss with her, life hasn't been easy. When I met her to interview her for a column, she had adopted the practice of leaving the country every year around Mother's Day, which is such a huge American holiday, otherwise she couldn't escape the painful reminders of her loss. She allowed herself to experience the loss when it hit her. Mostly, she trusted God to give her life continued meaning. He began to remind her that it had meaning simply because she lives and because he lives within her.

Your experience may not include a loss as devastating as this woman's, but whatever you are grappling with, know that God can and will see you through. Accept that as humans, we may not get all of the answers we want, or feel like we deserve, about why we must endure a trial or face an unfair circumstance. The answers we must cling to are those found in Scriptures, the ones that tell us that God will reward our faithfulness and our perseverance.

Our challenge is to view our situations as opportunities to grow closer to him so we can know his voice. God doesn't promise to make the process easy, fair, or fun. (I've moaned and complained about this on many a day!) What he does pledge, throughout Scripture, is his unyielding love: "Then you will call upon me and come and pray to me, and I will listen to you. You will seek me and find me when you seek me with all your heart" (Jer. 29:12–13).

He's not asking for blind obedience or calling for us to ignore our pain, our fears, or our suffering. He's calling us to remember that he is in the middle of it with us, and that despite what we see and feel, he does indeed reign forever, and his light will ultimately shine through all of the darkness. Walking more closely with him will help you find that light and make it part of your life.

Scripture

Psalm 30:5: Weeping may remain for a night, but rejoicing comes in the morning.

Prayer

Dear Father, sometimes the pain and evil all around me cloud my vision. I can't see you shining in the midst of this troubling storm. When I don't feel your presence or I question whether your hand is at work, help me to be still and know that nothing can dim the light of your son's shining love. When I find myself fretting over the injustices in this broken world, pull me back into your arms. Cradle me with your Word, and whisper into my heart that you are in control of the world and you witness every event. Help me to keep leaning on you even when I am left without rational answers. In Jesus' name I pray, Amen.

17

Your Red Sea Calling

If God told you to leave everything and everyone you love behind and move to the Red Sea, would you go?

A new friend asked me that question several years ago when our families took a weekend trip together. Our sons and daughters were schoolmates and had bonded, and it seemed this couple had quite a bit in common with me and my husband.

As the wife and I chatted one afternoon, she posed a series of questions raised in a bestselling book she and her husband often referred to over the years to spark conversation.* There were no right or wrong answers, but your responses helped others get to know you. The questions were fun and eye opening, and one in particular — the one I just shared — struck me as profound. When my friend asked it, I repeated it:

If God told me to leave everything and everyone I love behind and move to the Red Sea, would I go?

My friend said she had asked a man she was dating years

---

*Gregory Stock, PhD, *The Book of Questions* (New York: Workman Publishing Co., 1987).

ago this question and when he answered yes, she knew he was the one for her. They've been married for more than a decade. When she directed the question to me, I answered yes too. She, on the other hand, admitted that she wasn't sure what she would do; it would be a difficult choice.

Her honesty was compelling. It's easy to say yes, we would give up something we haven't yet been asked to sacrifice, or yes, we will always be faithful to God when that faith hasn't yet been tested.

Think about the apostle Peter, who never fathomed he would be ashamed of Jesus, and yet he denied knowing him three times (John 18:15–27). Think about the rich man who wanted to go to heaven, but not if it was going to cost him all that he had toiled for and accomplished here on earth (Matt. 19:16–24). I began asking myself if I were really any different. Are any of us any different?

Later that day, when this new friend and I were alone, our conversation veered to my career as a writer and how I routinely sacrifice time with friends and family to finish a writing project and to travel on occasion to promote my work. I told her how hard it was to leave my children, even for a couple of days, and how I take them along as often as possible. She listened and nodded, then mentioned our Red Sea discussion. Now, she said, she understood why I had answered yes.

"This is your Red Sea experience — your writing career."

I hadn't considered it in that light until she had that epiphany, but suddenly I agreed. Writing is my passion; it's a gift I've had since childhood. And yet, to write well and be sure that I'm excellently serving as God's vessel requires sacrifice, obedience, and time away to be quiet and still. I board airplanes more frequently than I would otherwise and spend more time on weekends spreading the good news that I believe God has inspired me to write in my works of fiction and nonfiction. If I don't write it and speak it, how will my gift be used to God's glory?

I recalled my dialogue with my friend a few weeks after that weekend getaway, when I picked up a book about the spiritual laws of success. Of course, most of us want to be successful, but God wants us to define "success" through his lens — not solely focused on material gain and professional accolades. God's measure of success is determined in the context of the number of lives we've touched with his love, often by meeting people's needs, whether as basic as food and shelter or as personal as friendship and social interaction. He measures success by noting how our walk with Christ has helped transform someone else's life.

With those tenets of success lodged in my mind, I read the bio of the woman who had penned the book and realized that her work was a "Red Sea experience" too. She had sacrificed something or experienced something that led her to share her knowledge on those pages. Rather than hoard the wisdom she had gleaned, she had decided to share her pain and victorious recovery to encourage others to persevere through challenges and claim their joy.

Sacrifice and calling often go hand in hand. Consider the life of voting rights activist Fannie Lou Hamer, or of Mother Teresa or Coretta Scott King. But this isn't really surprising. Wasn't sacrifice what God did when he sent us Jesus, and what Jesus did when he died for our sins? That same responsibility rests on the shoulders of each of us who write, sing, nurse, teach, care for children, intercede through prayer, or dedicate some other gift or calling to God.

Our Red Seas may not require us to literally relocate to another part of the world or even travel across our town. In our hearts, however, it's important to be prepared to go wherever God is leading.

Am I prepared? Will my answer always be yes?

I ask myself this occasionally, and like my friend, I don't always readily comply. When I find myself wavering, I view that as a signal to draw closer to God and ask him to bolster my faith and trust. I review biblical passages and devotional readings that remind me that he is with me wherever I go.

This question, if taken seriously, can help us determine where we are in our journeys of faith. It can be a good self-evaluation tool to help us focus on the big picture — God's omnipotent point of view rather than our human-sized vision of what we should be doing and where we should go.

What is your Red Sea calling? Are you ready to travel there with God? If you're not yet sure of your answer, ask God to show you why and to give you the courage to soon say yes.

Learning to Listen

Grab a journal or piece of paper and answer this question: *What is the one thing I would do, with or without pay, if I forced myself to stop making excuses?*

That, my friend, may be your passion, and this passion could be where God is calling you to serve. Ask God today to give you clarity on his vision for your life and the courage to pursue it. Don't be afraid; remember that wherever God leads you, he also journeys with you.

Scripture

John 12:23 – 26: Jesus replied, "The hour has come for the Son of Man to be glorified. I tell you the truth, unless a kernel of wheat falls to the ground and dies, it remains only a single seed. But if it dies, it produces many seeds. The man who loves his life will lose it, while the man who hates his life in this world will keep it for eternal life. Whoever serves me must follow me; and where I am, my servant also will be. My Father will honor the one who serves me."

18

Succeeding Scared

My friend Helena is an executive life coach who grew up in Switzerland, trained skating champions, and rarely uses the word *can't*. She's also a deeply spiritual person who believes that pairing a can-do attitude with confidence and faith can result in all kinds of miracles.

So when we met for lunch one day just after my third book had been released and she started spouting unusual, yet creative ways for me to promote my novels—ideas that would take me out of my comfort zone in some instances—she patiently listened as I explained why many of them wouldn't work, primarily because my children were young, and rather than have them grow up on the road traveling with me or grow up with me gone much of the time, I preferred to concentrate on less daring methods. Helena, the mother of two adult daughters, paused and looked deep into my eyes that afternoon. She asked a question I wasn't ready to answer, at least not to her, Ms. Glass Half Full: "You're afraid of success, aren't you?"

I denied that I was, but before I responded, I hesitated. We both knew that part of me was. Why? Probably more of

138

a fear of the unknown than anything else. I believe I was afraid that success might alter my ability to care for my family more than I felt comfortable with, and I didn't want to test any methods that would lead to results I couldn't change.

As usually happens with fear, my imagination had crafted all kinds of troubling scenarios without giving much thought to the wonderful possibilities. Helena went there, explaining that for every negative consequence there was always the potential for a positive one. She insisted I'd never know until I tried.

I eventually realized that, in part, I was hesitant to "blow up" because I wasn't sure some of the people around me could handle it. Would my excelling make them feel inadequate? Would I be treated differently by those close to me who didn't understand that my writing commitments weren't laid-back school assignments or a hobby? Would they understand that my occasional travel was part of the territory and join me in the endeavor or feel like I was leaving them behind?

I fretted about issues I couldn't control, until finally one day a year or so after acknowledging that I was indeed afraid, I had a conversation with a spiritual mentor who shared with me that she too had seen my hesitation. She explained that if I continued to shy away from allowing my writing gift to fully blossom, I would be resisting part of my God-ordained purpose. I needed to decide who would be my priority.

I learned during that assessment that part of the route to embracing the success God has for each of us is to first determine how we define success, because the way it is achieved and lived can be as unique as each person pursuing it. For me, I decided, it has to be intertwined with significance, which means not only do I want to excel in every area of publishing—with book sales, speaking engagements, and other opportunities related to my writing—I also want my work to stand for something and touch people in a way that can help transform their lives.

When I finally defined success as I desired it and stopped running from all that came with the call to write and be published, I was eager to be successful and significant, because I knew it would bring more attention to God for getting me there.

How do you view success, and what would it take for you to achieve it in your life? Does it mirror this world's perspective or God's? Have you asked God to guide you to the success he wants you to pursue?

As you answer these questions, consider, as I did, how Jesus defined success and how he achieved it in his own life. Jesus' view of success never echoed that of his biblical contemporaries and still wouldn't today. He despised what they idolized; they questioned what he cultivated.

He endured a bloody death on the cross, which to most who watched and mourned, meant that his ministry had ended in failure. Yet Jesus knew from the start that his public torture and death would be necessary to strengthen the belief in his victorious resurrection three days later. He asked the heavenly Father to give him the strength and resolve to move forward. He succeeded—on God's terms—for our sake.

Even when God grants you what many consider great

earthly success — wealth, power, and fame — he can surround you with fellow Christians to help you order your goals and your habits in a manner that keeps God as your first priority. When he blesses you in this fashion, it's not to make you boastful or prideful; it's an opportunity to show how even with all of your earthly treasures, you have decided to follow Jesus; you have decided that the trappings mean nothing without the Creator giving you wisdom on how to manage, and share, your wealth.

A vital thing to remember is that your success won't be the same as someone else's, so your route to achieving it likely won't be either. I think that's what Helena had been trying to tell me on that summer afternoon.

As your gifts and talents take you to greater heights, always make time to connect with God. Ask him to help you be a good steward over all he blesses you with. This wisdom will let you walk through that door that everyone else is afraid to open or may even let you create a door where one never existed. This wisdom will speak louder than your fear.

Time and time again, we must convince ourselves to do as Jesus did and adopt the discipline, courage, and sacrifices that come with aiming for success, while simultaneously embracing the blessings that come with obedience.

How do we do this? First, we make an honest assessment of what success would look like for us. Take some time to think, pray, and write down your idea of success from God's perspective. On that same sheet of paper describe your greatest fears. Is it fear of failure? Fear of others' reactions? Fear of change?

In a column across from your response to the question about fears, write down your worst-case scenario along with the positives that could result from your divine success. If you fear failure, what's the worst that could happen? The best? If you fear change, what's the worst that could happen? The best?

Now weigh the odds. Do the possible fears outweigh the potential rewards? Do you trust that as God says in his Word, he will grant you the desires of your heart, and that you can do all things through Christ who gives you strength? All things? Do you trust that he will protect you?

In essence, you have to decide that succeeding isn't an option, it's a must. A tragedy much worse than losing some friends along the way or stirring the resentment of people who put Christians under a microscope to look for flaws at every turn would be to stop before we reach our destiny and spend the rest of our days wallowing in regret over what we "could have" and "should have" accomplished. Jesus is watching and cheering us on. He is telling us to fear not, for we're more than capable of meeting the challenge and thriving under pressure.

Like Jesus, many of you won't measure success by your level of fame and fortune. The greatest yardstick will be the hearts you've touched and the lives you've seen improve as a result of allowing God to use you. Some of this generosity may never be publicly rewarded. But God knows, and his knowing is priceless.

Learning to Listen

After you craft the list detailed in this chapter, write the following affirmation in the same notebook or on the same page and recite it aloud:

Fear is not of God. I will succeed to bring God's name glory and honor and to draw others to God. I will excel in the areas in which he has gifted me, with gratitude instead of apology, determined to succeed however God defines success, even when I'm scared. I will listen so I can trust him. I will follow him so I can eventually lead.

Repeat this mantra every time you review your plan for success.

Scriptures

2 Timothy 1:7: For God did not give us a spirit of timidity, but a spirit of power, of love and of self-discipline.

Deuteronomy 31:8: The Lord himself goes before you and will be with you; he will never leave you nor forsake you. Do not be afraid; do not be discouraged.

19

Dancing to Life's Music

When was the last time you danced? Was it in the privacy of your home or at a public event with friends, family, or business colleagues? Did you let loose or contain yourself so inquiring eyes could not later incriminate you?

I ask this question rhetorically, because how you dance in public and private is likely an indicator of how you also share your heart and your faith. Like the women and men in biblical days who literally danced before God, or did so figuratively by serving him in other outstanding ways, we must find our signature move. These days, no one wants to be preached to or force-fed the message of Christianity or the Word of God. As St. Francis of Assisi is quoted as once saying, often the best way to spread the messages of salvation and faith are by how you live, talk, and treat others: "Preach the gospel at all times and when necessary use words." If your life is marked by peace, joy, generosity, and an abiding faith in the Master, you are dancing as unto the Lord.

Some of us literally can dance. We have a gift for footwork as elegant and sassy as the moves honed by contestants and professionals on the hit TV show *Dancing with the Stars*. Others of us have two left feet or two stiff hips, and the music just doesn't seem to cooperate. Whatever our skill level, we can decide to live in ways that reflect God's goodness, graciousness, and unconditional love. That's called dancing to God's rhythm. This doesn't take any natural talent; it simply requires us to choose what kind of life we want—one with joyful, God-centered abandon, or one overly constrained by the cares of this world, such as what we drive, where we live, and what we do for a living.

Just as determining what car, house, and vocation is appropriate will depend on who we are, so will choosing the right music and choreography for our spiritual dance. Our goal, therefore, is to know why we're dancing through life and for whom. We don't dance because we are without sin or because we have it all together; we dance because we can and because it is a form of praise to God for his unconditional love and for giving us blessings we haven't earned.

In 2 Samuel 6, the writer describes how David, who has been crowned king, is so thrilled that he finally is returning the ark of the covenant (which held the presence of God) to the temple that he danced in the streets with abandon. He didn't care who saw him or ridiculed him.

When his wife, Michal, questioned his actions, he defended himself by declaring that after all God had done for him, he would never regret his public praise. In studying this passage then, the question arises again, have you danced before the Lord, and if so, how?

Dancing here means loving God without self-consciousness—not attacking others about their lack of faith, waving a Bible, or demanding routine church attendance. Like the woman in Bethany, who washed Jesus' feet with her tears, wiped them with her hair, kissed them, and poured an alabaster jar of perfume on him to express her adoration and desire for forgiveness (Luke 7:36–50), our lives can serve as the same kind of heartfelt, surrendered offering.

Or consider the mother in 2 Kings 4, who went in search of the prophet Elisha after her young son's death. She didn't fret or weep; in fact she didn't give up on his life. She tracked down Elisha and told him, "It is well," even as in the next breath she explained that her son had died.

Certainly God calls us to fellowship with one another and to spread the gospel of Christ, but dancing is a personal form of worship. It is offering up to God the essence of who you are.

One woman I know "danced" before God by caring for her terminally ill ex-husband in the home they had once shared. Another "danced" unto the Lord by agreeing to serve as foster mother for a preteen pregnant girl and then agreeing to raise the baby too once it was born. Another woman does so throughout the year by providing mentors and free workshops to help struggling young mothers become better parents.

The beautiful thing about the dances we can offer in praise to God is that they come after we've been redeemed, after Jesus has died for our sins and provided the eternal sacrifice. This means we don't have to wait until we're perfect or blameless. We can dance right now because his grace and mercy abound.

What kind of dance does your life exemplify? Are you trusting God with the eagerness that the woman with the alabaster box and oil possessed? Are you worshiping and serving with this kind of abandon?

Dancing like this is a lifestyle. It develops as you know God better and learn to discern where he is leading. It is choreographed with years of love and patience and by trusting God with all your heart. A song that was popular a few years ago said of life, "If you get the chance to sit it out or dance, I hope you dance!" I hope you'll dance too.

Learning to Listen

Read Luke 7:36–50 and 2 Samuel 6 to learn what led the woman with the alabaster jar of perfume and King David to dance. Ask yourself in what areas of your life you could be more daring and open to new ideas, new people, and new opportunities. Jot down a few ideas and, in prayer, ask God to guide you toward what to tackle and when, and to give you the strength to dance through the process with joy.

20

Living Courageously

ourage. When you read this word or hear it, what comes to mind? For me, there are a series of images—the fire-fighters who tried to save people trapped in the World Trade Center after the terrorist attacks of September 11, 2001; the pilot who safely landed an airplane on New York's Hudson River in January of 2009 without losing a single passenger; the cowardly lion in *The Wizard of Oz*.

Yes—the lion. This animal captures my attention in a reflection on courage because for the longest time, it baffled me to think that such a large and majestic creature could be scared of anything. The lion possessed everything he needed to thrive—tremendous strength, a powerful roar, and the respect of the other animals just because of his hierarchy in the jungle.

What he lacked, however, was even more meaning-ful: the ability to move forward in spite of his fears. Simply put, that's all courage is anyway. It requires summoning a strength you may not know you had, and using it to be strong and wise on someone else's behalf or for the greater good.

Role models not only abound in our world, but tons exist in the Bible. Numbers 27:1–5 recounts the story of five sisters whose father, Zelophehad, died, leaving them with no male heirs. The daughters of Zelophehad found the courage to stand before Moses and other leaders to ask for their father's property. In biblical times, men owned property. Without a brother to inherit what had been their father's, they would have nothing if their bold request were denied: "Why should our father's name disappear from his clan because he had no son? Give us property among our father's relatives" (Num. 27:4).

Then there was Abigail, who in 1 Samuel 25 is described as an intelligent and beautiful woman married to a wealthy, foolish man named Nabal. While David and his men were living on the outskirts of the city of Carmel, they protected Nabal's servants as the servants sheared sheep. When David and his men began to run low on supplies, they sent word to Nabal, asking for whatever he could spare. Nabal insulted David and refused to give him anything. An angry David decided to kill Nabal and all of the men in his house.

One of Nabal's servants informed Abigail, who quickly made a plan. She gathered as much food and drink as she and her servants could carry and went in search of David. This act alone was courageous for a woman during biblical times, when men had to grant permission for their wives to travel. Imagine her approaching an angry David and his four hundred men. She could have been killed on the spot. Instead, she dismounted from her animal, fell on her face, and begged forgiveness for her husband's foolishness.

We need the type of courage possessed by these biblical women to manage our modern-day dilemmas. We need to know when to stay put and when to step out on faith, trusting that what we see doesn't always have to be what we accept.

Discernment about when to act and when to stand still doesn't surface just because we ask God to grant it. Courage won't appear overnight and seep into our pores while we sleep. It is developed through effective communication with God, the kind that requires routine prayers and regular efforts to recognize God's responses.

Sometimes the answers come while we're studying Scriptures because God's instruction or belief about an issue was given to Christians of long ago. At other times, we need to listen more and talk less to determine what he's calling us to do in a particular circumstance. If you have asked for guidance, he will provide it. As we mature in our relationship with God, we'll become wiser in trusting when to wait on him to fight our battles or provide justice, and when to arm ourselves with his promises and secure justice in his name.

The daughters of Zelophehad and Abigail moved forward out of necessity. They stepped outside the norm for their gender and their culture to secure their future in one instance, and to save her family's life in the other. That took faith and courage.

The Bible indicates that Moses took the request of Zelophehad's daughters to God, and God told him to honor what they asked because they rightly deserved what had been their father's. From that day forward, property laws changed to indicate that women could receive the inheritance left by their father if their father had no living sons.

God also blessed Abigail by allowing David to soften his heart to her pleas. He did not kill her or her family, and when Abigail's foolish husband died ten days later, David married Abigail and made her part of his family.

Your challenges may be unusual, or your fear may seem insurmountable; but rather than give up hope, remind yourself that courage isn't the absence of fear; it's summoning enough strength to move forward anyway. The blessings awaiting you when you do can be life-changing.

Learning to Listen

Memorize the following verses and recite them whenever you find yourself in a period of doubt or fear.

Haggai 2:5: "My Spirit remains among you. Do not fear."

Deuteronomy 31:6: "Be strong and courageous. Do not be afraid or terrified because of them, for the Lord your God goes with you; he will never leave you nor forsake you."

21

Follow Your Leader

Jesus wasn't known as an extrovert who oozed charisma or impressed everyone he encountered with polished social skills. However, biblical accounts of his life on earth reflect a man whose quiet demeanor was magnetic.

If anyone could be boastful and confident, it should have been him. He was the Son of God; he possessed the ability to heal the sick, raise the dead, and perform countless other miracles. People flocked to him like modern-day groupies now follow basketball and rock stars.

Yet according to the few biblical stories we have about his appearance, Jesus was rather unassuming—not noted to be strikingly handsome like David or Samson. Whatever his physical stature, he had no desire to impress others or receive special treatment. Because he knew who he was and whose he was, a certain peace and self-assurance cloaked him. He didn't need credentials to make a statement; his mere presence and the spirit of God dwelling inside of him spoke volumes.

Jesus' inner light made him the kind of guy who, once you got to know him, you wanted him as a friend because he was so real. He treated everyone with the same regard — women and men, young and old, poor and wealthy. When he spoke, he fed people. His wisdom was so rich and helpful to the soul that once it was nourished, little else mattered.

Jesus also didn't waste time trying to convert or secure the approval of people who made light of his ministry or held him in disdain. If the Pharisees wanted to see what he was up to, they could visit the public places in which he was holding court, but he didn't actively seek them out or try to redeem himself in their eyes. He let his sermons and deeds speak for themselves, trusting that God would justify him and protect him.

One of the most powerful examples he set for us was his routine guarding of his energy. He showed us exactly what to do to regain our focus and our balance on a regular basis. He retreated by himself for lengthy periods to pray and be alone with God.

Sometimes he invited a few disciples along, but often he had them wait nearby while he communed with his Father. This quiet time of retreat was a period when God filled him, just as we now need, with an infusion of God's love, power, wisdom, and might.

Imagine your car's gas tank hovering near empty as you race to make it to an important meeting on time. You squeak into a parking space just in time to ride the elevator to the proper floor and slide into your seat before the session begins.

Afterward, however, you have to coax your car to make it two more blocks to the nearest gas station. It chugs along and sputters as you pull to a stop in front of a pump. Didn't you whisper a relieved "Thank you, Lord!" as you got out to fill the tank?

The sound of the fuel chugalugging through the hose and into the gas tank reminds you of a thirsty sports player guzzling a fortified beverage during time out. When the tank is full and you start the car, it's as if the vehicle has breathed a sigh of relief. Does it seem easier to steer and increase your speed?

The spiritual walk that Jesus so perfectly modeled for us is much the same. When we're filled with the Word of God, we navigate life's twists and turns with more ease. We don't always have to protest loudly when we're mistreated or fight for ourselves when we're misjudged. Instead, we can recall the scriptural declarations in which God calls himself our defender and protector (Ps. 91). (So is the Holy Spirit, who dwells in us and is certain to intercede on our behalf.)

Jesus never allowed his gas tank to run too low. He knew how and when to refuel and never felt guilty about taking the quiet time or finding the space he needed to regroup. He knew if he didn't keep himself connected to the source of his divine strength, he'd have nothing to share with others.

That kind of dwelling with the Father—the kind that keeps me silent when I'm tempted to say too much, still when it seems I want to work my way into heaven, and disciplined about making quiet time for God—is a daily goal, a process I'm seeking to develop, as much as is humanly possible. If anyone is guilty of over-scheduling and trying to squeeze in just one more worthwhile task, it's me. I thrive on keeping active, but there have been seasons when I've had to acknowledge my pace was too intense. I needed more silence in my life.

I'm reminded when those periods creep upon me that I probably got myself into the predicament because I wasn't tuned in as properly as I should have been to what God wanted me to put on my agenda and move to the forefront at that time. It's also during these seasons that I realize leisure time shouldn't be optional, for without adequate down time, during which we can quiet our minds and get away from the chatter of the world's opinions and the clutter of everything else that seeks to persuade us one way or another, we can be unguided ships, bobbing along on a whim of the wind, without remembering that the God who controls the wind and the rain and even the high seas is looking out for us.

At the same time, we need to be looking for God too. We can't do that unless we follow Jesus' example and regularly refuel our spirits and souls. Habakkuk 2:20 declares that all the earth should be silent before the Lord. The ways in which we can accomplish this are as unique and individual as we are. Some do it through meditation, others through more formal prayer. Others simply seek silence.

I've informally practiced each of these methods, but when my life is the most hectic and I find myself stuck in the car more often than not, traveling from one work-related endeavor to another or transporting my children to and from school activities and practices and programs, I've found it valuable, once I'm alone, to get alone. By that I mean to not make phone calls as I'm prone to do from my cell phone, to not pick up a book or magazine that I'm carrying because I've been longing to read it, and to not turn on the radio or play a CD.

I sit or drive in silence and let my mind wander. At first it's unsettling. I feel like I'm wasting time. But just about every time I go through this process and allow myself to simply be, God speaks to me. He gives me clarity on an issue I've been wrestling with or drops a surprise piece of inspiration into my heart and mind that otherwise I would have been too scattered or distracted to receive.

I marvel every time it happens, yet I shouldn't. By now I should expect to hear from him, knowing that because I'm giving him my full attention, I also have his. That's what Jesus modeled for us in his everyday life. We can't match his perfection, but in reaching for it, with every attempt we become closer to God and more like God.

Learning to Listen

Find at least ten minutes three times this week to sit in silence. Ask God to speak to your spirit as you rest in him. The first three, four, or even five times, you may do nothing but focus on the pace and depth of your breathing. But soon, as your mind wanders over the events of your day or settles on an issue that has caused you to fret, God may speak a truth to you.

Don't go into this experience expecting revelations or answers. Simply invite and expect his presence. He will speak how and when he desires. In the meantime, you will grow comfortable with the practice of retreat that Jesus modeled. He was a CEO who wasn't a workaholic. We don't have to wear that human badge of honor either.

part 4

Hearing God

As I've said throughout this book, God won't knock you over with his message; but his feather-light touch and loving presence won't go unnoticed if you're paying attention to yourself and to your soul. The more you get to know him, the better you'll recognize how he speaks. Just as you know the habits and tastes of your parents, child, or spouse, you'll learn what makes God smile, ticks him off, or sends him into protective mode on your behalf.

Once you make the decision to communicate with God more fully—where you not only pray but also listen for his guidance and his will for your life—begin studying his Word and looking for him to speak to you in both simple and creative ways. Embrace the truths about who you are and get quiet enough for God to start a dialogue with you.

Sometimes you'll feel his presence like the mighty rushing wind described in Acts 2:2. At other times, you'll feel a faint uneasiness or confirmation in your spirit that signals to be still or go forward.

Hearing from God is exciting. I'm still learning all the time the different ways in which he wants to reveal himself to me. And just as each of us is unique, so are the ways in which he chooses to make himself known to each of us.

That's the beauty of this journey. Walking with God will continuously make your heart go pitter-patter. He'll show up in surprising and inspiring ways and never leave you doubting that he stopped by. Open your ears, your heart, and your eyes and expect to be transformed.

22

Trusting That Voice

A recent springtime Saturday morning errand turned into a mini-tour of the metro area in which I live because I didn't trust myself.

I was visiting a particular suburb to which I rarely venture, and I needed to mail a package. I was familiar enough with the area to remember that I had passed a post office on a nearby road at some time in the past, yet I wasn't certain of its exact location.

My quick fix for the problem was to rely on my car's navigation system. I reached the intersection that I suspected led to a post office, but I hesitated because the navigation system didn't note that a facility was nearby. For a split second, I considered following my instincts and turning right. Instead, I listened to the monotone instructions supplied by the female navigation "pilot" and made a left, which led me onto a route that I questioned at every new turn.

Fifteen minutes later, when Ms. Navigation instructed me to take the interstate to reach the closest post office location visible on her map, I knew I would be traveling too far out of the way. I made a U-turn, determined to find the post office I had encountered before.

Sure enough, I found it near my starting point. I had been just seconds away when I sat at that traffic light and second-guessed myself. I couldn't see the post office from the road, but it had been less than a block from the intersection.

The moral of this detailed description of my directionally challenged escapade is this: the more we trust ourselves, the more we'll learn to trust the source of our being, who is our ever-present guide. The more we listen to our internal positioning system, the more likely we'll find ourselves where we're destined to be.

Everything we need is already within us. God has given us the smarts, the talents, the gifts, the compassion, and even the guidance of the Holy Spirit to help us navigate the terrain we must cross to fulfill our purpose. Often, however, we doubt what's right in front of us. Just like I figured that the robotic voice in my car (that in hindsight didn't have the most up-to-date mapping software) knew better than I did how to get me where I needed to go, we rely on other people's advice and opinions to tell us who we are and what should serve as the focus of our lives. All the while, something inside of us is protesting as we go along to keep the peace or support the team.

I made it to the post office that day about five minutes before closing time because I'd taken such a wandering route. I was minutes away from being too late. Thankfully, God's grace is sufficient. Thankfully, he gives us new mercies everyday and more opportunities than we sometimes deserve to self-correct.

Imagine, however, if we compensated for our cloudy

knowledge by regularly talking to God and trusting the God in us. We'd have far fewer worries about taking wrong turns or missing closing deadlines, because we would believe the first answer that God poured into our spirit was the right one. Reaching that level of spiritual insight is a process. Each lesson learned is another step in the right direction.

In my case, the next time I begin to question my know-how or even my memory, I'll give myself the benefit of the doubt before placing my trust elsewhere. I'll remember that God is my personal navigation system, intent on getting me to the right destination and fulfilling my ordained purpose right on time.

Learning to Listen

Recall a time you second-guessed yourself and wished you hadn't. What made you doubt? Why did you ignore that inner voice? With these answers in mind, vow to respond differently the next time a circumstance arises in which you're led to listen to yourself. Follow the Holy Spirit's lead, then note the outcome.

Scripture

Psalm 19:7–9 (MSG):

> *The revelation of God is whole*
> *and pulls our lives together.*
> *The signposts of God are clear*
> *and point out the right road.*
> *The life-maps of God are right,*
> *showing the way to joy.*

The directions of God are plain
    and easy on the eyes.
God's reputation is twenty-four-carat gold,
    with a lifetime guarantee.
The decisions of God are accurate
    down to the nth degree.

23

Recognizing His Will

When God gives you a vision, do you map out your plan and create a timeline for making it your reality, or do you leave those steps to him? A friend recently posed that question as she wrestled with what God would have her do next with her life. She has spent more than a decade in a career with comfortable pay and job security, but for nearly half of that time, she has felt herself being led toward an endeavor that could make a huge difference in a lot of young lives.

How, she asked, would she know for sure what God was calling her to do? Should she wait for him to give her a sign or move forward as if her "feelings" were an answer?

I suggested that she do both. James 2:20 tells us that faith without works is dead. If she sincerely believes that God is calling her to focus her energy and abilities elsewhere, why not knock on a few doors to see where they lead? While taking that approach, she also should be praying every step of the way, asking God for wisdom, for favor on the paths he wants her to take, and for doors that it's not time for her to walk through to be closed.

This may sound both simple and complicated, yet it's a concept that works. When God is orchestrating your future, he can subtly slow the pace of a course you're raring to chart or shift into high gear a promising opportunity that you've given little thought. It's important, for those very reasons, to have regular quiet times with him and to be in tune with how he speaks specifically to you. The way he's calling you to respond may not mirror the action he asks your sister-friend to take.

As the old gospel song says, "What God has for me is for me." Certainly he sometimes speaks in widespread messages or signs, but often because he tries to develop a special relationship with each of his children, God will speak to you in ways that fit your personality and level of trust, and ways in which you'll hear him best.

For Comfort Anderson-Miller, it took a simple glance. In 2005, she made her annual mission trip to her native Liberia to deliver school and medical supplies and other helpful goods to the struggling residents of her war-torn homeland. During a stop in a small town, she saw a small young boy with large, sad eyes standing in the crowd, gazing at her.

She was startled, because he had a gaping hole in his face where his nose and upper lip should have been. She knew that the beliefs in Liberian culture mirrored those of biblical times, meaning this child was likely being shunned because of his disfigurement. He wouldn't go to school or make many friends or have a productive life if he stayed where he was, in the condition he was in.

Comfort didn't know his name or who his parents were, but God told her that day what this mission trip had really been about: to see this child and find a way to help him. She would find his parents and get their permission to bring him to the United States for medical treatment.

The road from making that decision to bringing it to life wasn't easy. Comfort made calls and sent letters to medical professionals to find a plastic surgeon willing to perform facial reconstruction on the boy for free. As she worked on securing his medical services, her mother, who still lived in Liberia, helped her locate the child and find out more about his family.

Comfort learned that his name was Edward Sando and that he was the youngest of five children. He had been bitten by some type of insect while his family hid in the bush from warring rebels. By the time his parents sought medical care, his nose and upper lip had become dangerously infected. Doctors had to remove the nose and upper lip to save his life. He was two when this happened and five when Comfort discovered him.

By the time she secured the help of plastic surgeon Jonathan Jacobs and oral surgeon Joseph Niamtu, Edward was six. He arrived in the United States filled with enthusiasm and delight at coming to a country with running water, electricity, and more food than he had ever seen.

Within a year, he had undergone several surgeries and had a reconstructed nose and upper lip. His outgoing personality and gratefulness for a new chance at life won him many friends in his local community. Comfort made it her mission to instill an understanding in him about the importance of the gifts he had been given. She and her husband eventually adopted Edward, with his birth mother's consent. That move allowed him to stay in the United States and attend school and gave Comfort an opportunity to assume a role she had never given much thought to: motherhood.

Her obedience to God's beckoning meant that Edward would be the only one of his five siblings to receive a formal education. It meant that under her guidance, he too would learn to love and praise God and listen for his leading. Edward recently graduated from high school and intends to become a chemist, if not the president of Liberia some day. For now, both he and Comfort thank God for sending her to Liberia when he needed a savior and for Comfort having the courage to keep knocking on doors until she found the help he needed.

Learning to Listen

Can you remember a time God has spoken to your spirit and directed you to do something? Maybe he nudged you to make a call or say a prayer or encourage someone. Did you dismiss that feeling as something fleeting or did you follow through? Ask God to give you the wisdom to know when he is speaking to you and the courage to obey, even if what he's asking seems daunting.

24

Listening in the Valley

Spring is my favorite season, specifically the month of May, because it's not too steamy and the April rains have ceased. What I enjoy most are the colorful sprays of blooming flowers that can be found just about everywhere, from landscaped business lawns to neighborhood yards. The different varieties and shades are ever-present reminders of God's love of beauty. Simply put, they make my heart smile.

In March and April, when I'm struggling not to complain about overcast skies and unpredictable weather, I have to remind myself what's coming. If I can endure the windy, rainy period, I'll be rewarded by frequent bursts of sunshine and the blossoming of those flowers I cherish. I urge myself (and others) to think like that when we find ourselves experiencing some personal rainy days or windy seasons. Because we don't know what lies around the bend, we can only hope that the wind and rain are pit stops in a valley.

Valleys are those deep and unexpected dips or ditches along life's path that one can't always control. They are cliffhangers that have the potential to devastate you. When you're in that deep and sunken place, you have to decide not to let it trap you. You have to be still and allow God to save you.

Shadrach, Meshach, and Abednego were in a valley — actually a blazing furnace — where they easily could have been consumed. Instead of panicking, they recalled the promises of God and remained calm. They waited for him to determine their fate. The miracle God performed by joining them in the furnace and then sending them out (without one hair on their heads being burned) led even the king to profess a desire to serve God (Dan. 3).

Yet God doesn't always save the day, heal our loved one, or grant the miracle we were determined to witness — at least not from our perspective. Sometimes the words God speaks to us in our darkest hours serve as reminders to accept that God's will is greater than our desires and that it is best. When I look back at the times in my life that were the most painful or difficult, I can see how he used those experiences to mature me and to draw me closer to him.

I didn't have to wait until later to grasp that message one morning in the spring of 2005. My mother died on the same day that year that Pope John Paul II went to heaven, and God revealed himself to me in ways I'll never forget. Mama had been sick for a couple of weeks but suddenly took a turn for the worse the night before. I was en route to the airport to catch a predawn flight to Arkansas where she lived, when one of my sisters called with the news. Mama had died just a few hours earlier; I hadn't made it home in time to check on her or sit at her bedside before she breathed her last breath.

I was devastated, and I wept so bitterly as my husband drove me the last few minutes to catch my flight that my daughter, then a first grader, began praying in the backseat, asking God to comfort me.

Through the blur of my tears, I somehow grabbed my suitcase and stumbled into the airport to my airline's check-in area. And that's when God began to speak. Over the next six hours, he would send me sign after sign that he felt my heartbreak, understood my anger, and wouldn't leave or forsake me.

It started with the airline attendant who took me aside when she saw me struggling to check in with my credit card. She retrieved my boarding pass for me and asked me what was wrong. When I explained that my mother had just died, she asked me just the right question: "Did your mother know the Lord?" When I nodded, she squeezed my hand and smiled. "Then it's going to be alright; she's with Jesus now."

She checked my bag, then sent me on my way, toward the security gate that led to the terminal. But before I had gone two feet, I ran into an older woman, a member of the church I attended. She saw my red eyes and trembling lips and embraced me. I told her my mom had just died and she grabbed my hands and reassured me: "You know what our pastor says: Absent from the body, present with the Lord." And then right there in the middle of that busy airport terminal, with people swirling all around us, she prayed with me.

I was surprised when I boarded the plane an hour later to discover that Ms. Stith and I would share the first leg of our flight. We both had layovers in Houston on the way to our final destinations. Had I not been in such pain, I might have been stunned when I realized that her airplane seat was right across the aisle from mine. She didn't bother me as I alternated between gazing out of the window and shedding tears, but her presence was comforting, because I knew I could lean on her if I needed her.

As we were leaving the plane, she grabbed my hand and squeezed it again. She looked me in the eyes and declared with confidence, "You are going to be alright." She said it so fiercely that I believed it, though I felt just the opposite at that moment. I wouldn't learn until two weeks later, when I returned to Richmond, that Ms. Stith was not only about the same age and height as my petite mother, she also was named Dorothy—my mother's first name.

I got off the plane in Houston, thankful that I'd made it closer to home, but drained by all of the emotion. While I sat in the waiting area trying to control my tears, I decided to check my cell phone. There was one message waiting for me, from my friend Kim, who knew I had been contemplating a visit home to my mother. She had urged me to go and when she called my office that morning and didn't get an answer, had accurately assumed I was on my way to Arkansas.

She didn't know when she left the message that it was one I needed to hear. Kim wished me well on my journey and quoted the New King James version of 2 Corinthians 4:16: "Though our outward man is perishing, yet the inward man is being renewed."

How had she known? I became certain that God was with me in this valley, speaking to me and assuring me that while he had to fulfill his will for my mother's life, he was mindful of what this loss meant to mine. Though I knew this meant she was out of pain, no longer needing kidney dialysis or daily medicine or fretting about other aches and pains, I hadn't been ready to release my only parent. My kids were just six and three; I still needed her guidance. While I was an adult, at thirty-two I still had many years during which I could have benefitted from her wisdom.

But as God spoke to me that day through friends and strangers, when I didn't know how I'd survive the pain, I somehow knew that he would guide me.

He delivered his final reassurance that afternoon when I arrived in Arkansas where my three sisters solemnly greeted me and took me by Mama's house. I can't recall why we ventured into her bedroom; probably in search of something we'd need for her funeral. What caught my eye was the large-print Sunday school lesson she had been reading around the time she had left home to go to the hospital.

Because this was Lenten season, the forty days leading up to Jesus' crucifixion and resurrection, the Scripture and accompanying text on the page she had left open focused on the Son of God. What took my breath away was the title of the lesson: "Victory over Death." I heard God loud and clear.

There would be many days that spring when I cried as the rains fell in April and felt comforted by the sunshine in May, but what saw me through my darkest moments, including when my aunt, my mother's only living sister, died twelve days later, was the memory of the day God took Mama home and spoke directly to my need.

He used people, Scripture, voicemail, and even a Sunday school lesson title to let me know he was not only going to hold my hand; sometimes he was going to carry me through. I heard him, and I was thankful.

Prayer

Dear God, you alone know when I need to hear from you and how best to get your message through. When I'm in a valley filled with pain or find myself struggling with loss, help me remember that you are near to the brokenhearted. Help me remember that you are my comforter and if I will listen for you, I'll hear your words and messages of comfort. Every life must experience rain; when I am soaked, let me trust that you will always send the sunshine and sometimes even a rainbow. Amen.

25

Soaring

Do you remember what you wanted to be when you were five years old, or maybe slightly older? Can you recall the pride and excitement you felt whenever an adult asked and you could emphatically state that someday you would (fill in the blank)?

Whatever season of life you find yourself now enjoying, it's likely that you recall your childhood dreams. I remember my early fantasies of Diana Ross–like stardom before my love affair with the written word took hold, and I still smile now when I recall the declarations offered by my two children when they were that age.

My daughter initially wanted to be a dentist before, in recent years, deciding that life is leading her toward the more glamorous route of acting. As an elementary-age student (with a four-feet-eleven-inches-tall mother), my son is determined to play professional basketball for a decade before retiring and launching a career as a surgeon.

Few of us discourage our young children when they come to us with these grand designs to do great things. And why should we? If you can't dream without abandon and create a world of your choosing in childhood, when there are no stakes involved, will you ever again be untainted by the obligations and demands from society that compel you to color within the lines and to follow the status quo?

Certainly, some do take risks later in life and pursue their passion without regard to stability and what others think, but traveling this less-worn path doesn't come naturally in a society that measures success and worth by your bank account balance and job title.

I find it interesting that in contrast to this heavy emphasis on wealth or the prestige of one's career, the greatest man who ever walked the earth was a modest carpenter. Jesus had the connections and the aptitude to do whatever he wanted, yet he chose a profession that put him on par with less affluent and less revered men, one that required him to use his hands to work and, in essence, to serve, his clients. In the end, the work he did became a metaphor for his entire ministry: just as he sawed and shaped wood to construct something from nothing, so he cuts away and molds and transforms those of us who learn to follow him.

Until we reach the maturity to seek him, though, we grow from a position of bright-eyed enthusiasm, trusting and believing that the world is ours for the tackling. When life assaults us, through death or some other form of loss, through broken families and strained relationships, through illness or betrayal, it's easy to get off and stay off track. It's easy to lose our way and stay stuck. We begin to let others or society dictate our choices, and we stop dreaming lofty dreams, the kind that would allow us to soar above the clouds, as eagles do. Instead we stay grounded out of fear, low self-esteem, or the inability to fly solo. If we want to hear from and follow God, however, it's important to begin framing that all-important question of what you want to be differently, in a way that can be life altering for even the youngest of responders.

Instead of asking what do you want to be, we should be asking our children and ourselves, *who* do you want to be? By asking *who* instead of *what*, the first thing we're doing is asking a question that cuts to the core of who we are as a person, to our character instead of just our work or our actions.

While *what* you want to do may be firefighting, *who* you want to be allows you to be faithful, courageous, loving, kind, and honest. You can serve in any capacity and still be a servant of Christ, still be a woman that pleases God. Who you want to be can lead you straight to Christ, and in finding him, discover more of who you are in the first place.

It's critically important to understand that the God we serve never intended to clip our wings and ground us. The purpose he gave each of us, regardless of whether it's celebrated by others, is enough to help us soar.

Eagles soar because they have wide wingspans that lift them high above the wind. They also possess excellent eyesight, with which they can assess a situation and quickly act. And while they sometimes travel together, eagles aren't afraid to soar alone.

The patterns and practices of eagles serve as a guide for where God wants to take us. When we steep ourselves in prayer and in his Word, he lifts us above the conflicts and pressures that could otherwise take us down. While our physical eyesight may be questionable, when we pray for his wisdom and the ability to discern beyond what the physical eye can see, God grants us the insight to navigate pitfalls that threaten to deter us.

We women are wired to be in fellowship with others. We want to spend time with friends and family; we love to be part of our community, whether it be church, work, or our neighborhood. To think of isolating oneself from that, even temporarily, can be worrisome. That's where we need to trust that wherever God wants us to fly, he's leading the way.

Whether we do so physically or simply by having our own private prayer space, a place to go and talk to God on a regular basis, we have to be prepared to soar toward the destiny God is placing in our hands. Everyone can't go where God may be leading you, and sometimes even if others join you, there's a particular part of the journey that God wants or needs for you to travel alone.

In Genesis 21, Abraham sent away his wife Sarah's slave, Hagar, and the son Hagar had borne for him at Sarah's insistence. When Hagar ran out of food and water in the desert, she began preparing herself and her son to die. Yet God heard her cries and reassured her she wasn't alone; he would provide for her. A spring of water appeared before her in that dry land and Hagar's faith was renewed. God spoke to her and told her to return home; he would see to it that she wasn't harmed. Had she not traveled this frightening and painful road alone, Hagar might not have encountered the Lord, and she might not have been in a position to hear him. Her story illustrates the need for trust as we listen. God uses both our faith and our attentiveness to lead us into our destiny.

The Creator is speaking to each of us just as he spoke to his chosen people thousands of years ago. He's urging us to trust him, to allow him to carry us on eagle's wings, so that we can fly high above everything that's weighing us down and keeping us from thriving.

Isaiah 40:30–31 says, "Even youths grow tired and weary, and young men stumble and fall; but those who hope in the Lord will renew their strength. They will soar on wings like eagles; they will run and not grow weary, they will walk and not be faint."

The charge and mission are clear. We first must hope in the Lord to always uphold us, and to always be there to help us be who he's calling us to be, as long as we abide in him and live according to his Word.

Our task then is to concentrate on renewing our strength whenever it falters. We must believe that God will take us where he wants us to go and give us the energy and stamina to succeed. The key is to stop focusing on what we want to be and start declaring who we want to be for Christ, in every area of our lives. At any age, we can decide to be a woman willing to soar to new heights for Christ.

Learning to Listen

Write a list of what you want to accomplish at this stage of your life. Then write a companion list of who you want to be — i.e. honest, patient, giving, etc. Pray over both and ask

God to give you eagle-like wisdom and sight, and the ability to soar above pitfalls toward the destiny he desires for you. In all of your asking, be sure to ask God to help you be real, with him and with yourself; to be still, so you can hear and see him at work; and to be in tune, so that you never lose communication with him and can hear his voice when you need to most.

26

Whispers to Your Soul

If you had a chance to special order a conversation with God, what criteria would you include? Would you ask him to summon you in a particular language or call you by a certain name? Would you want to take notes or record the conversation to listen to again later?

Of course, we can't "package to suit" our relationship with God or the divine manner in which he speaks. And truthfully, would we really want to? By trying to box the all-knowing God into our limited human parameters, we would be compromising his willingness to manifest miracles and wondrous solutions in our lives. By putting conditions on the conversation, we'd be indicating that we knew more about what would meet our needs than he, our divine Creator.

The decision to tune in to God's whispers is a choice to surrender to his agenda. God is ready and willing to whisper to the souls of his children who are living according to his commandments and seeking to reflect the fruit of the spirit. Certainly we will falter; but because God knows our hearts, he is willing to help us get back on course.

Sometimes, however, it's comfortable to take the easy

way without realizing that what should be mere support has become a crutch. I, for example, adopted the routine of calling friends to pray for me or offer spiritual guidance whenever I confronted a troubling issue.

What did she think: Was I handling it the way God wanted me to? Did I need to repent — again?

In theory, there's nothing wrong with seeking support from fellow believers. The Bible says the prayers of the righteous are powerful and effective (James 5:16), and that where two or three are gathered, Christ is there as well (Matt. 18:20).

However, one afternoon when I made a call to a friend and she wasn't home, I paused then and there and talked to God about what was troubling me. I shared the pros and cons with him, just as I had planned to do with her. I realized in that moment that my seeking support was becoming a habit, and maybe even a burdensome one.

I put myself on a fast from asking for feedback or advice from people who may have genuinely wanted to help, and in doing so found myself listening more closely for other ways in which God might be speaking. I gained clarity on new ways to hear him, and at the end of the process, felt closer to him and more confident about my ability to hear that still small voice, through which he speaks, inside me.

These days, whenever I feel worry sneaking upon me or I began questioning how to handle a situation, I still seek knowledge and wise counsel, and sometimes even prayer, from others. But my first strategy is to pray myself — for wisdom, guidance, patience, and of course, for answers.

The answers don't always surface immediately, but by freeing my mind and changing my pattern, I have given God an opportunity to do what he does best—surprise me and bless me in ways I never could have imagined. I have learned that if I remain patient and open to hearing from him, he will always respond. The answers come in his timing, not mine, though. And God often delivers them in subtle forms—through a gentle tugging to follow his lead, a perfectly-timed comment from a friend or mentor, or an amazing opportunity that only God could have orchestrated.

While I'm waiting for him to whisper my name, I have learned to be comfortable with silence and to sometimes simply allow my spirit to be quiet, so that I can hear him. When I recognize his voice, I'm eager to respond, and sometimes I even break into a song.

Scripture

Psalm 107:28–30: Then they cried out to the Lord in their trouble, and he brought them out of their distress. He stilled the storm to a whisper; the waves of the sea were hushed. They were glad when it grew calm, and he guided them to their desired haven.

Prayer

Heavenly Father, thank you for being a divine Creator who loves me enough to communicate with me. Thank you for giving me opportunities to know you better and serve you more. Lord, please speak to my heart and whisper to my soul how I can be more pleasing in your sight. I long to hear from you, both when I'm wrestling with day-to-day issues and when a big decision looms. I appreciate the prayer partners and other wise counsel you continue to surround me with, but please keep guiding me individually as well. Thank you for your continued favor and for allowing me to walk with you through life. Amen.

Final Word

Dear Friend,

Wherever you find yourself right now — in a solid place of fullness and peace, or in the turbulent seas of uncertainty or heartache — I pray that this book has helped you realize that God is your friend and he wants to experience life with you. He is ready and willing to communicate with you, as soon as you invite him to do so.

I hope this book has guided you through periods of questioning or storms and reminded you of the times that God held your hand or carried you. If you are currently facing difficulties, please know that you don't have to face them alone. The God within you is greater than whatever is seeking to rage against you. Call out to him today and ask him to reveal himself to you.

God isn't an outdated historical figure who only spoke and performed miracles during the lifespan of Moses and his mother, Jochebed, or during Ruth's or Mary's day. He is still speaking today, to our hearts, to our minds, and to our spirits. We have to focus more intently than ever to hear him, but he declares in his Word that if we seek him with all of our heart and soul, we will find him (Deut. 4:29).

I know this to be true, and I pray that if you aren't

already certain of this fact, that you soon will be. Return to this book often, reading the sections in whatever order best suits your particular need, and ask God to use these pages as one of his instruments to help you become a better listener and grow closer to him.

Make the practices outlined in this book part of your regular routine:

Find the courage to take a good look at your life and decide whether it's pleasing to God and to you;

Make time to get quiet and be still on a routine basis, so God can dwell in your spirit and speak to your heart; and

Follow where God leads you, remembering that he knows your end before you've even begun, and if he has blessed it, you will be blessed.

When you decide to make him a priority, you'll find yourself desiring other things less. An unintentional pruning will begin. And slowly but surely, the voice of God will become stronger and more recognizable.

Godspeed and God's favor upon you as you give God the chance to grace your life with his living Word and with his whispers of love, purpose, and truth.

Yours in Christ,
Stacy

Acknowledgments

Every book a writer pens is like one of his or her babies, and this project is no different. What makes this one especially precious is the fact that this is my first work of nonfiction.

I'm honored to have had this opportunity to share from my heart in a book that was birthed because of the vision of my editor, Sue Brower. Sue, thank you for planting the seed for a book that I pray helps our sister-friends (and us) deepen our relationship with God. Many thanks to Becky Philpott, Karwyn Bursma, and the Zondervan sales team for championing this book.

I also am grateful to my agent, Steve Laube, and to the women—both named and unnamed—who allowed me to share their stories in this book. They include Polly Chamberlain, Shon Gables, Arnecia Crawford, and Comfort Anderson-Miller.

Sincere thanks are offered to my husband, Donald, and to our two children for their continuous support, and to my siblings, Barbara Grayson, Henry Haney, Sandra Williams, and Patsy Scott, and other extended family for being part of my village and helping me carve out the space and time to write. Your tangible help, thoughtfulness, and prayers are a gift that I don't take for granted. I especially thank Charmaine Spain, Carol Jackson, Muriel Miller Branch, Connie, Ernest, and Marisa Lambert, the Murphy family, Bobbie Walker Trussell, Edward Sando-Miller, Gwendolyn Richard, Barbara Rascoe, and my church family for your assistance and prayers. I also thank book clubs, bloggers, and booksellers who support this work and readers everywhere for journeying with me down a path that I hope has made you stronger, more hopeful, and eager to live your life and your faith at a new level.

Last, but certainly not least, I thank my late mother, Dorothy A. Hawkins, who taught me how to let God lead and to listen for his direction, and most importantly, my heavenly Father, for allowing me to be one of his vessels, penning books and speaking the Word in a manner that I pray will draw all women (and men) to him.

Bible Versions